preschool
parties

easy ideas
for princesses, pirates
and other little people

Colleen Mullaney

sixth&spring books

sixth&spring books

161 Avenue of the Americas, Suite 1301
New York, New York 10013
sixthandspringbooks.com

Managing Editor WENDY WILLIAMS
Senior Editor MICHELLE BREDESON
Book Design JOY MAKON
Layout MICHELLE HENNING
Photography JACK DEUTSCH
Editor ERIN SLONAKER
Copy Editor KRISTINA SIGLER

Vice President, Publisher TRISHA MALCOLM
Creative Director JOE VIOR
Production Manager DAVID JOINNIDES
President ART JOINNIDES

Library of Congress Cataloging-in-Publication Data

Mullaney, Colleen, 1966-
Preschool parties : easy ideas for princesses,
pirates and other little people / by Colleen Mullaney.
p. cm.
Includes bibliographical references and index.
ISBN 978-1-936096-17-6 (alk. paper)
1. Children's parties. 2. Preschool children. I. Title.
GV1205.M85 2011
793.2'1--dc22
2011012220

Manufactured in China

1 3 5 7 9 10 8 6 4 2

First Edition

Acknowledgments

Thanks to all my little party people, who endured cold mornings, rainy days and numerous costume changes with big happy smiles, all for a little cake. Allie, Amelia, Amélie, Annabel, Carter, Clare E. G., Clare P. G., Coco, Dilan, Everett, Grace, Hugo, Isadora, Jack M., Jonah, Jordan, Katherine, Maggie, Max, Meredith, Nicholas, Pete, Ruby, Zachary, and especially to my Jack, who finally got to be a pirate!

I owe a great deal to my photo guru Jack Deutsch, who is willing to play with puppets and spaceships to get the magic shot.

Thanks to my friend Alissa, who graciously offered her house as party central—and is still cleaning up the sprinkles.

Annie, your confections and cakes were both beautiful and delicious.

Huge thanks to Bets, whose grounding force was instrumental in producing this beautiful book. From prop master to caterer, she did it all.

Hugs and kisses to my own little party people, Grace, Katie and Jack, who lived through the madness of the mudroom-turned-crafting-center, the cakes and cupcakes everywhere, and the crazy long days of shooting. We did it!

Thanks also to my team at Soho, who agree that when a child's party is made magical, the memory will last a lifetime.

contents

INTRODUCTION

Most of us look back fondly at the birthday parties of our childhood: simple celebrations with cake, ice cream, a party hat and a game or two. The cake was the highlight of the party, a moment everyone looked forward to—the kids because of the sugary treat and the parents because it signaled the end of the party. Cake, a quick song, and then, balloon in hand, out the door you happily went.

Fast-forward to today. When it comes to organizing parties for our own children, many of us don't have the confidence to do it ourselves. Working as well as stay-at-home parents are under tremendous time constraints, and any extra time is devoted to other pursuits, not planning or worrying about how to create an elaborate party your child will love.

This book is a must-have for these parents! I know that the first foray into preschool party hosting can be extremely daunting, but I make it easy. Planning a basic themed party is a perfect way to create those priceless memories your little one deserves. It also gives you a chance to get to know your child's friends.

You may be thinking, "I don't have time now. How will I pull this off?" The answer is that it's easy if you have a plan and keep it simple. I promise, you will enjoy the experience as much as your child. Kids are easy to entertain and have very attainable expectations. With the fuss-free, accessible ideas in this book, I'll help make your party planning a breeze.

The parties are geared for kids from ages 1 to 5—from the very special first birthday and toddler years to the bigger Pre-K kids, with tasty treats everyone will love. The games and activities are easy but will keep everyone engaged, busy and happy. Whether they are digging for dinosaur fossils or creating a fairytale wand, it's all fun. Each of the 15 colorful, themed parties includes ideas that take you from start to finish: invitations, setting the scene, activities, menus, and lastly, creative cakes, of course!

Step-by-step directions make it easy to whip up a memorable party. All of the supplies and ingredients I've used can be found at your local crafts or grocery store. But no pressure: This book is meant to be a helpful guide for parents who are planning a birthday party for the first time, or parents that are looking for more colorful, creative ideas for their little one's birthday party. So, read on and let the party begin!

pretty in pink

fairy land

Fairy parties are a perfectly magical way to celebrate your little girl's big day. Just picture a room full of sparkly little fairies dancing about in a pastel-rainbow, dreamlike setting, and you're sure to smile. This delightful party features easy crafts and games and delicious delicate treats sure to please. It's a truly enchanting party your little sprite will never forget.

fairyland

SCHEDULE

Duration:
Approximately 1½ hours
(2–3:30 p.m.)

2:00–2:30	Craft wands and crowns
2:30–3:00	Snacks and games
3:00–3:30	Fairy Wand Cakes and more games

Invitations

A plain white piece of construction paper and a bright pink foamy sheet is all you need for this darling invite. Start by gluing the paper to the sheet. Using a star cookie cutter or template, trace a star shape on the white paper and cut out the stars. In bright pink marker, write all the party information such as date, time and place. Turn the star over and have your child adorn the star with the adhesive gems. For added charm, punch a hole at the top of the star and thread a length of decorative ribbon through.

Setting the Scene

Start by creating an enchanted fairy bower, which, as fairy lore states, is a magical retreat for tiny sprites. The hideaway—a hula hoop frame covered in layers of pink tulle—hangs like sugared icing on cupcakes (use tape or glue to adhere it). Puffs of pink tulle blossoms and ribbons add the finishing touches. Hang the bower from a tree, patio overhang or trellis so that it has plenty of room to drape freely. If the party is indoors, hang it from a hook in the middle of the party space. Party treats, such as star-shaped cake pops and pixie punch, are perfectly sweet set on a table by the bower. Magical wands, sure to be a hit with your fairy guests, are easy to make ahead of time or during the party as another festive activity between fairy games.

TO DO

Beforehand

- Craft the bower, flower ball and jeweled crowns.
- Make the Fairy Wand Cakes.

Day of

- Clear the party space and hang the bower.
- Decorate the birthday girl's chair with a length of tulle and tie with a bow to secure.
- Hang the flower ball on the chair back.
- Set the table with crafty wand supplies.
- Frost and decorate the Fairy Wand Cakes.
- Make Fairy Bread and Pixie Rolls.
- Mix up the Fairy Punch.

Supplies

FOR THE INVITATIONS

- 8 sheets white construction paper
- 8 pink foam sheets
- Glue
- Pencil
- Star template or cookie cutter
- Scissors
- Pink marker
- Adhesive gems in various colors
- Hole punch
- ¼-inch satin ribbon

FOR THE PARTY

Fairy Bower
- 1 36-inch hula hoop
- 10 yards ⅜-inch-wide pink satin ribbon
- 3 yards ⅜-inch-wide bright pink grosgrain ribbon
- 10 yards light-pink tulle
- 6 yards medium-pink tulle
- 6 yards raspberry-pink tulle
- 1 package faux rose petals in shades of pink
- 1 6-foot pink faux rose garland
- 10 yards 1/2-inch-wide pink satin ribbon

Fairy Wands
- 8 pink foamy wands
- 6 sheets of adhesive gems in pinks and purples
- 2 stems faux mini daisies
- Glue sticks

Fairy Flower Crowns
- 12 feet of wire-based gemstone garland
- 8 yards ¼-inch-wide satin ribbon in shades of pink
- 2 stems pink faux sweet peas

Flower Fairy Blossoming Ball
- 1 faux rose-covered ball
- 2 faux peony blossoms
- 10 faux light-pink rose blossoms
- 1 stem variegated ivy
- 1 yard ⅜-inch-wide pink grosgrain ribbon
- Floral pins or hot glue gun and glue sticks

fairyland

Party Time

Have your guests dress in their fairy best—they'll be more comfortable in their own tutus and tops. When they arrive, treat them to darling bejeweled headpieces, which are easy to make and add a lot of glamour to any outfit. Wrap lengths of decorative jeweled garland (found in the wedding aisle of your local crafts store) into circles and tie on lengths of ribbon. These are also great goody bag or take-away favors. So much better than candy!

The little girls will be plenty entertained with a few games and all the tasty snacks. Dressing up is most of the fun!

Game Time

All of these fairy games are short and fun. Prizes need not be expensive. Stickers, small change purses or colorful notebooks are always popular with the fairy set.

GUESS HOW MANY

YOU'LL NEED: A jar; candy to fill it; small prizes (if desired)

Fill a jar with pink candies or beads for this classic game. The children guess how many are in the jar. The fairy with the closest number to the correct amount without going over wins the contents of the jar or another prize of your choice.

LIMBO DANCING

YOU'LL NEED: A long pole or broom handle, music, small prizes

Play some fun tunes (see page 142) to set the mood. Have two adults hold the pole between them at waist height. Line the fairies up and have each limbo dance under the pole. The pole is lowered after everyone has a pass. Fairies that touch the pole while going under it are out of the game. The fairy who goes the lowest under the pole without touching it is the winner!

FAIRY GODMOTHER SAYS

YOU'LL NEED: Your own crown or wand; a wand for each fairy; small prizes

This game is both fun and short, so it's perfect for little ones' limited attention spans.

This is the fairy version of Simon Says. The adult, wearing a crown or holding a wand, directs the children to do as the fairy godmother says. For example, "Fairy Godmother says to touch your wand to your nose."

The fairies that don't touch their wands to their noses are eliminated or out of the game because they didn't do what the Fairy Godmother told them to do. The last remaining fairy is the winner.

fairyland

FAIRY PUNCH

3 cups fresh strawberries, hulled
and quartered
¼ cup fresh lemon juice
1 cup sugar
2 liters sparkling water
4 cups ice cubes

Puree the quartered strawberries in a blender or food processor. Strain the puree through a fine-mesh sieve, pushing the solids through with the back of a wooden spoon, into a pitcher or punch bowl. Add the lemon juice and sugar and mix well. Just before serving, add the sparkling water and ice cubes.

FAIRYLAND MENU
Fairy Bread
Fairy Punch
Pixie Rolls
Fairy Wand Cakes

FAIRY WAND CAKES

1 yellow or chocolate cake mix
(recipe page 140)
Pink frosting
Colored sugar sprinkles
Lollipop sticks

Follow the recipe on page 140, or prepare from a box. Bake cakes in a small silicone star baking pan. Let cool. Decorate with pink frosting, then add fairy sprinkles. Let set. Insert lollipop stick into bottom of star halfway through, lengthwise, and serve.

PIXIE ROLLS

¼ cup strawberry jam
¼ cup raspberry jam
6 slices white or whole-grain bread,
crusts removed
Pink sugar sprinkles

In a small bowl stir the jams together. Spread the jam mixture evenly on one side of the bread and roll each slice up. Place roll on a cutting board seam side down, and cut each roll in half crosswise. Place seam side down on a decorative plate or platter and sprinkle lightly with pink sugar. TIP: For a thicker roll, add ¼ cup softened cream cheese to the jam mixture before spreading on the bread.

FAIRY BREAD

12 slices white or whole-grain bread
Unsalted butter at room temperature
or vanilla icing (page 140)
Colored sugar sprinkles
Butterfly-shaped cookie cutter

Cut a butterfly from each bread slice. Spread with butter or icing and top with sprinkles. Serve.

ahoy matey!

sail the high seas

A high seas adventure is easier to create at home than you might think. With an innovative pirate ship as a base, these little bootleggers will have a merry old time!

ahoy matey!

SCHEDULE

Duration:
☠ Approximately 2 hours ☠
(11 a.m.–1 p.m.)

11:00–11:30	Make telescopes
11:30–12:00	Treasure hunt
12:00–12:30	Lunch
12:30–1:00	Cake and games

Invitations

A simple white skull and cross-bones design (see template at the front of the book) on black cardstock will instantly set the party theme. Invite guests to "Walk the Plank" or "Sail the High Seas" with the birthday boy or girl.

Setting the Scene

Transforming a jungle gym, swing set or outdoor play area into a pirate ship takes just a few bucca-neering items like a sail, flags, ropes and a wave or two. A string of Jolly Roger flags were made from black and white felt and the skull-and-crossbones template. The main sail was rigged from a piece of canvas and a plastic flag from a party store. If the canvas has clean edges, pull a few threads on the ends to get a frayed effect. Tied onto the ship with rope, it looks rough and authentic.

Rolling waves are cut from cardboard with sharp scissors and painted with poster paints. We leaned them against the jungle gym so they would stand up. Scary skull accessories are made from inexpensive paper mache molds from the crafts store that have been painted white with black eyes. (Keep these decorations to use again at Halloween!)

TO DO

Beforehand

- Prepare and freeze ice cube trays with fruit punch and grape juice.
- Make the flags and sail.
- Make the waves.
- Bake Pirate Cake.
- Gather costumes.
- Set the party table.
- Fill treasure chest.

Day of

- Prepare the food and drink.

Supplies

FOR THE INVITATIONS
- Cardstock in white and black
- Markers

FOR THE PARTY
- 10 sheets black felt
- 10 sheets white felt
- Scissors
- Glue or adhesive spray
- Tape
- Canvas fabric, for sail
- Flag
- Rope
- Cardboard
- Poster paint in blue, white and black
- Paper mache skulls
- Black foamy pirate hats
- Eye patches
- Red bandanas
- Face painting kit
- Foam swords
- Stuffed parrots

Telescopes
- Empty paper towel rolls
- Black poster paint and brushes
- Pirate-themed stickers
- Glitter markers

ahoy matey!

Party Time

Dressing up as a pirate is the first part of this entertaining party.

Costumes for the looting bunch were easy to make. I asked the kids to wear their own striped T-shirts and blue jeans that we rolled up. A quick raid of your own closet (and a call to the other parents) can yield old white shirts, jackets and ties, or find these items at a thrift store. The black foamy pirate hats, eye patches and red bandanas are all found at the crafts store. These make great take-home gifts.

After a few swipes with some face paint, even the most innocent little faces can look like looting bucca-neers. Parents should handle the face painting so the situation doesn't get unruly! A few foamy swords and stuffed parrots make for authentic high seas style.

Telescopes are easy to craft and can occupy the pirates for a bit. Give each kid an empty paper towel roll, paint, lots of stickers and glitter pens. Write each kid's name on the inside edge so there's no confusion, and let them dry while they're playing the various swashbuckling games and eating the treats!

Game Time

TREASURE HUNT

YOU'LL NEED: Wooden box; play jewelry, candy and other treats to fit in the box; paper; tea bags; markers

What pirate-themed party would be complete without a treasure hunt? Fill a wooden box with play jewelry, candy and other treats and hide it well! Make a treasure map of the area, giving areas seaworthy names. For example, bushes could be "the rapids." Make your map look old by dyeing it with tea. Give the kids the treasure map and let them go on the hunt! Once they find the loot, they can claim their booty.

WALK THE PLANK

YOU'LL NEED: 2-by-4 length of wood; bricks; inflatable crocodiles and other creatures; small prizes

More of a balance game than anything, this game is so much fun for the little pirates, they end up "walking the plank" many times!

Set up two small stacks of bricks and place the 2-by-4 "plank" across them. Have it raised so that the plank is about one foot off the ground (you don't want kids to hurt themselves if they fall!). Set the inflated crocodiles and creatures on either side, lurking in the "water" below. The goal for the kids is to race across the plank without falling off! Give prizes to each kid that makes it across safely.

ahoy matey!

Pirate Menu
Captain's Crunchy Chicken Strips

Blackbeard's Guacamole and Chips

Pirate's Treasure Punch

Pirate Ship Cake

PIRATE'S TREASURE PUNCH

- 8 ounces fruit punch
- 8 ounces grape juice
- 3 1-liter bottles lemon-flavored seltzer

Fill ice cube trays with fruit punch and grape punch and let freeze. When ready to serve, fill a plastic drinks dispenser or punch bowl with the seltzer. Add the juice ice cubes and serve.

BLACKBEARD'S GUACAMOLE AND CHIPS

- 2 ripe avocados
- ¼ cup chopped onion
- ⅓ cup chopped tomato
- 2 teaspoons chopped fresh cilantro leaves
- 1 teaspoon lime juice
- Tortilla chips

Cut, peel and chop the avocados, removing brown pit. In a blender or food processor puree the avocado, onion, tomato, cilantro and lime juice. Scoop into a serving bowl. To keep the guacamole from discoloring, push avocado pit in the center of guacamole until ready to serve.

CAPTAIN'S CRUNCHY CHICKEN STRIPS

- 3 pounds chicken tenderloins
- 8 ounces plain yogurt
- ¼ cup creamy ranch dressing
- 3 cups corn flake cereal, crushed

Preheat the oven to 375°F. Rinse the chicken and pat dry with paper towels. In a bowl, combine the yogurt and ranch dressing. Pour the crushed corn flakes into a bowl. Dip the chicken in the yogurt mixture to coat well, then roll the strips in the crushed flakes. Place on a baking sheet and bake for 30 minutes or until cooked through.

ahoy ☠ matey!

PIRATE SHIP CAKE

Embellished with flags printed from the computer raised up on bamboo skewers, this cake gets high marks on the high seas and makes for jolly pirates indeed!

3   batches vanilla or chocolate cake
    (recipe on page 140 or 141)
1   batch vanilla frosting
    (recipe on page 140)
Blue food coloring
2   batches chocolate frosting
    (recipe on page 141)
Assorted candies, such as Kit-Kats,
    Tootsie Rolls, strawberry laces
    and grape sour balls
Pirouette biscuits
Ice cream sugar cone
Fondant in yellow
Silver dragees

Bake three 9-by-13-inch sheet cakes according to directions on page 141 until a toothpick comes out clean. Let cool, then remove from pans.

To the vanilla frosting add two drops blue food coloring and stir until blended. Set aside in a covered bowl.

Set one cake layer on a piece of cardboard covered in foil or a large platter. Coat the top with a layer of chocolate frosting. Place another cake layer atop the first and add a layer of chocolate frosting. Cut the third cake layer in half; place one half along the back of the cake to form the aft deck. Cut a 4-inch strip from the rest of the third layer and place it at the front of the ship.

Using the photo as a guide, cut the cake's sides to round the back and create a point for the bow in the front. Discard the cut-away parts. Frost the entire outside of the cake with chocolate icing.

Decorate the cake with the candies: Tootsie Rolls for railings, strawberry laces for rope, a pirouette cookie as the main mast. I made the crow's nest by lightly frosting the bottom portion of an ice cream cone and pierced it with a bamboo skewer that stood inside the pirouette cookie. I made treasure chests by cutting open Tootsie Rolls and covering the inside with yellow fondant strips to mimic gold and silver dragees to look like silver coins. Grape candies stuck together with frosting look like cannonballs.

Kit-Kats cut and placed upside down in a pattern make up the mid-deck planking. To finish, roll the yellow fondant into a long strip to accent the sides of the ship. Use the blue frosting on the platter or cardboard to form the sea, and this ship is ready to sail!

arty
paint*a*licious
party

This party is sure to be a
colorful affair. With some quick and
easy materials, a little space and some
imagination, you can draw out the
artist in every child. Painting
and crafts are great activities for kids
of all ages and can provide
endless ideas for your child's next
birthday masterpiece!

25

# arty party

SCHEDULE

Duration:
Approximately 2 hours (12–2 p.m.)

12:00–12:30	Painting
12:30–1:00	Pizza
1:00–1:30	Games
1:30–2:00	Cupcakes

Invitations

Invitations shaped like artist's palettes are a great way to inspire your child's friends and get them excited about the coming celebration. Cut a palette shape from white poster board and glue different-colored buttons, paper circles or stickers for the paint colors. Use the space in the center to write out the party details.

Setting the Scene

Create a lofty open "studio" space for the artists by moving furniture and rolling up any rugs. For an indoor party, hang an expanse of white butcher paper on the wall or across the windows with tape. If the party is outside, hang kraft paper (a large-sized crafting paper that is usually either white or brown and comes in rolls or sheets) along a fence, patio posts or side of the house. Gather the paints, brushes and markers and have them close at hand on a butcher-paper-covered table. Keep wipes nearby to clean little fingers and, of course, have a trash bag handy.

TO DO

Beforehand

- Make or buy the cupcakes and gather supplies.

Day of

- Clear the party space and hang the large paper canvas.
- Cover the tables (and the floor, if necessary) with butcher paper.
- Arrange tubs of paint and bins of brushes, markers and pencils on the table.
- Set smocks and wipes out so they are ready for little artists.
- Fill paint tins with color-coded snacks.
- Prepare the veggie platter.
- Prepare mini pizzas with sauce and toppings, place them on baking sheets, cover, and have the oven ready.
- Set out the toppings for the cupcake decorating station.
- Mix up the punch.

Supplies

FOR THE INVITATIONS

- White poster board, for invitations
- Buttons, paper circles or solid stickers
- Glue
- Markers

FOR THE PARTY

- Roll of white kraft paper
- Roll of butcher paper
- 10 1-inch foam brushes
- 8 16-oz. tubs of water-based paint, in a variety of colors
- Art smocks, one for each artist
- Markers, in a variety of colors
- Baby wipes
- Plastic cups
- Empty paint tins, for snacks
- Empty picture frames, one for each artist

✳ arty party

Party Time

This party is all about the painting—and creativity. Protective gear is essential when little ones paint! I picked up inexpensive artist's smocks at the crafts store. Have everyone don a smock, then load each kid up with a plastic cup of paint and let them claim a spot at the canvas. Let them discover the artist within!

When painting time is up, it's time for dessert! To let the little artists' originality shine through, instead of a cake, put out plain cupcakes that can be decorated while the canvas dries. A homemade palette platter (cut out of white foamboard) holds the different candies for decorating, each in its own colored cupcake liner. Give each child a cupcake that's been frosted with plain white icing to decorate further!

When the canvas is dry, cut a section from each child's work and frame it to make a meaningful keepsake. I picked frames up from the crafts store.

Game Time

After standing and sitting and painting and doodling, these games work great with this age group, who might need a diversion.

WHAT AM I?

YOU'LL NEED: Small prizes

This is a fun thinking game revolving around colors. The kids guess what object you are by to your clues and your answers to their questions.

All the players sit in front of the leader—you or another adult—and you begin with a clue. For example, if you are the sun, say, "I'm yellow." If one of the kids guesses "Are you a banana?" you can say, "I'm bigger than that," and then give another clue, such as "I'm hot." Keep going like this until one of the children correctly guesses what you are. In keeping with the artist theme, pick different-colored objects for them to guess, and give the winners small prizes such as crayons, markers and sidewalk chalk.

FREEZE DANCE

YOU'LL NEED: Small prizes

This is a truly classic children's game that is ideal for the younger set as they dance away their energy.

Choose some entertaining children's music (see page 142). When the music plays, the kids must dance! When the music stops, the children freeze, remaining perfectly still until the music starts again. Anyone that moves is out of the game. The last child remaining is the winner.

 arty party

SNACK TIME

Snacks in red, green, yellow and orange served in clean, unused paint cans or buckets keep the artists going strong. This is a fun way to get creative with your child—find ways to color coordinate their favorite snacks. The cans, which are found at paint or crafts stores, can be used after the party to store art supplies or small toys.

ARTY PARTY MENU
Colorful Snacks in Paint Cans
Mini Pizza Palettes
Veggie Sticks
Sparkling Cranberry Punch
Decorate-Your-Own Cupcakes

DECORATE-YOUR-OWN CUPCAKES

18 cupcakes frosted with vanilla icing (see recipe for cake and frosting on page 140 and 141)
Mini marshmallows
Rainbow-colored sprinkles
Various candies such as Skittles, M&M's, mini gummy fish, jelly candies

Allow the kids to decorate the tops of the cupcakes with whatever candies they choose!

MINI PIZZA PALETTES

1   12-ounce tube frozen pizza dough, thawed, or one fresh ball of dough
1   cup tomato, pizza or marinara sauce
12   cherry tomatoes, sliced
4   cups shredded mozzarella cheese

Preheat the oven to 425°F. Divide the dough into 8 pieces. On a lightly floured surface, roll each piece into an 8-inch mini round. Spread 2 tablespoons of sauce on each round, then sprinkle with ½ cup cheese and top with cherry tomatoes. Transfer to a cookie sheet. Bake for 10–15 minutes or until the crust is golden brown and the cheese is melted and bubbling.

SPARKLING CRANBERRY PUNCH

48 ounces lemon-flavored seltzer
16 ounces cranberry juice
16 ounces lemonade
2   lemons, sliced
4   cups ice

In a plastic drinks dispenser, combine the seltzer, cranberry juice and lemonade. Add lemon slices and ice, mix well and serve.

VEGGIE STICKS

10 carrots
3   cucumbers
6   celery stalks
30 string beans
30 cherry tomatoes
2   each red, orange and yellow peppers
Ranch dressing, if desired

Wash and dry veggies. Peel the carrots and cucumbers, and pull the strings from the celery. On a cutting board with a paring knife, slice the carrots, cucumbers, celery and peppers lengthwise into sticks. Arrange on a platter with whole string beans and tomatoes. Serve ranch dressing on the side in a small bowl, if desired.

under the big top!

it's a circus!

What do birthday parties and the circus have in common? Lots, starting with fun and games for kids who love a good time! Why not combine the two for a most memorable party? Bright colors, carnival games and tasty snacks keep kids busy and engaged. And with easy planning and setup, parents will also delight in this fresh and festive celebration.

33

under the big top!

SCHEDULE

Duration:
Approximately 2 hours (12–2 p.m.)

12:00–12:30	Face painting, hat decorating and puppet shows
12:30–1:00	Games
1:00–1:30	Lunch and more games
1:30–2:00	Cupcakes

Invitations

Take a sheet of red-and-white-striped scrapbooking paper and cut out a 5-by-8-inch rectangle. Trim one 5-inch edge with scallop-edged scissors. With stripes facing down, fold the scalloped edge over to half an inch from the other edge. Write the invitation text on the blank inside of the card with colorful pens or markers.

Setting the Scene

Decorating a colorful circus decor takes a bit of planning, but it will definitely be worth it. Our party was held outdoors, but if you are planning your party inside, start by transforming the room: Create a tent effect with paper streamers hung from the center of the ceiling—or use fabric in the same way. Tape lengths of streamer to the center of your ceiling, then drape it to the side wall and tape it at the corner, then allow it to fall to the floor. Repeat for many more streamers until the ceiling is covered, mixing up the colors so the effect is colorful and fun.

  Every circus has a ringmaster, high wire act and strongman. Painting a large piece of cardboard with one of these figures using acrylic paints makes a fun vignette for your young partygoers. Cut out the face, and partiers can become these characters! Have each child pose for pictures as the character! E-mail the pictures to the kids later.

TO DO

Beforehand

- Make the Strongman vignette.
- Hang the streamers to create the "tented" room.
- Gather props and old clothes for dress-up.
- Gather hand puppets and set up a stage, if desired.

Day of

- Bake cupcakes.
- Make Popcorn Balls.
- Prep Pigs in a Blanket and have oven ready.
- Mix up the lemonade.

Supplies

FOR THE INVITATIONS

- Red-and-white-striped scrapbooking paper
- Plain scissors
- Scallop-edged scissors
- Ruler
- Pens or markers

FOR THE PARTY

- Paper streamers or fabric
- Tape
- 1 tri-fold cardboard presentation board
- Acrylic or poster paints
- Brushes
- 1 foamy sheet in a blue glittery finish
- 4 buttons
- Craft glue
- Large foam sheets in a variety of colors
- Pom-poms in assorted colors
- Glittery craft gems in assorted colors
- Stapler or hot glue gun
- Face painting kit
- Puppet show stage
- Hand puppets

under the big top!

Party Time

Gather old clothing—maybe all the parents can help out by bringing an assortment—so kids can make their own costumes. It's great to see what crazy combinations they pull together. Make it an activity by setting up a station and applying face paint to willing little clowns. Many of the hats and circus accessories I had were found in party and crafts stores or were dug out of closets at home. Headpieces were crafted from feathers and gems glued onto elastic hairbands, while pompoms and crepe paper gave basic foamy hats a spectacular finish.

The hats were crafted from foamy sheets cut and stapled into cones, decorated with pom-poms and colorful paper streamers for trim. If time allows, craft a bunch of bases and have the kids decorate their own circus hats.

Let the children demonstrate their showmanship by performing a puppet show for their friends using hand puppets. We purchased a puppet show stage from a game store, but you could cut and decorate a wardrobe box and hang a curtain across the top if you wanted to make it yourself. Set cushions or mats out for audience seating. Give each willing child a try, but help them with a story line or prompt them with ideas to get them started. Give a prize for the funniest or most dramatic show.

Game Time

Circus games are easy to pull together, whimsical, and most of all, fun!

CLOWN FACE PAINTING

YOU'LL NEED: Face painting kit; chairs

Good face painting kits are available at party and crafts stores; get one with lots of colors and brushes. You don't have to be an artist to apply face paint! Basic shapes of hearts, butterflies and stars work great, as do painted-on tattoos. For full clown faces, paint noses and lips red, cheeks white, and add designs. This takes a bit more time, so only work up clowns if you can get some help with face painting from an older sibling or another parent.

SHOOT THE CAN

YOU'LL NEED: 10 empty soda cans; water guns; small prizes

Line 10 empty soda cans along a table or ledge about 2 yards away. Give each child a water gun filled with water, and line the kids up in a row, one child in front of each can. Say, "Ready, set, go!" and let them start shooting. The first one to knock over his or her can is the winner. (Tip: Although I pick the first five kids as winners, I also always have smaller prizes handy for all the kids, so everyone wins. Remember: small people, big feelings.)

PING-PONG TOSS

YOU'LL NEED: Ping-pong balls; plastic buckets; small prizes

Place plastic buckets about 2 yards from the kids in a random pattern. Put a handful of small prizes inside each bucket. Line the kids up and hand each child 3 ping-pong balls. Give them 3 chances each to get their balls in the buckets—any successes mean choosing a prize from the bucket.

under the big top!

CLOWN CUPCAKES

18 vanilla cupcakes
(recipe on page 140)
1 tub vanilla icing (or 1 batch
recipe on page 140)
18 sugar cones
½ cup each blue and red
decorative sugar
1 tube decorative blue
icing fitted with star tip
Skittle candies
M&M's Minis
Red gobstopper candies
Red licorice
Orange Twizzlers

Bake the cupcakes according to recipe on page 140 and allow to cool. Frost the cupcakes with vanilla icing. Make clown hats by covering the sugar cones with more icing and rolling in red or blue decorative sugar. Press hat firmly into top of cupcake. Put a dollop of icing on the point of the hat and add a Skittle to finish. Make faces by adding M&M's Minis eyes, red gobstopper noses and red licorice mouths. For hair, cut 1-inch pieces of orange Twizzlers into strips and press into place. Make a collar by piping the blue frosting around the base of the cupcake.

Big Top Menu

Popcorn Balls
Pigs in a Blanket
Classic Lemonade
Clown Cupcakes

POPCORN BALLS

12 cups popped popcorn
Vegetable oil
2 cups sugar
¾ cup light corn syrup
½ cup (1 stick) butter
¼ cup water
1 teaspoon vanilla extract

Place the popcorn in an oiled bowl. Cover two spatulas with oil and set aside. In a saucepan over medium heat, combine the sugar, corn syrup, butter and water. Insert a candy thermometer and boil the mixture until the thermometer reads 260°F. Remove from heat and stir in vanilla. Pour over the popcorn and mix until well coated using the spatulas. When cool enough to handle, form into small, fist-sized balls.

PIGS IN A BLANKET

8 hot dogs
1 package crescent rolls

Preheat oven to 350°F. Cut the hot dogs into thirds. Roll out the crescent dough on a smooth surface. Separate a triangle piece of dough and cut it into thirds, then wrap one section around a piece of hot dog. Repeat with the remaining dough and hot dog pieces. Place on a baking sheet and bake for 10–12 minutes or until golden brown. Serve.

CLASSIC LEMONADE

1 cup sugar
1½ cups freshly squeezed lemon juice
6 cups cold water
3 cups ice

In a pitcher, mix the sugar and lemon juice together until the sugar is completely dissolved. Stir in cold water, add ice and serve.

garden ❀ party
flower power

This is not your garden-variety party! Create a birthday girl's dream garden with flowers, games and treats that will delight all of her senses. A flower-themed party isn't difficult or expensive to pull off indoors or out, making it ideal any time of year.

garden party

SCHEDULE

Duration:
Approximately 2 hours
(11 a.m.–1 p.m.)

11:00–12:00	Games
12:00–12:30	Lunch and cupcakes
12:30–1:00	Piñata time

Invitation

Our handmade flower invitations get little girls in the mood! For each invitation, cut 7 petal shapes from various colors of cardstock. Cut one 1-inch diameter circle (for the center). Punch a hole at the narrow end of petals and in the center of the circle. Stack the petals and place circle, lining up the holes, and secure the stack together with a paper fastener (brad). Open the petals up and use a marker to write the party details on each petal, with the main message in the circle. You could say, "See how I've grown!"

Setting the Scene

Colorful flowers dominate this party's decorations. The table is our centerpiece: Set out a cheerful tablecloth and pile it with cupcakes and brightly colored pails overflowing with play jewelry and candies for take-home treats. Instead of a planter of real flowers, I filled them with lollipops that the girls could pick themselves!

To make the "flower" lollipops, cut a leaf collar (see template at the front of the book) from a foamy sheet, punch a hole in the middle and slide it up the lollipop's stick—be sure to have one for each guest. Set them out in a clean planter so they appear to be growing: Styrofoam cut to size in the bottom of the planter, covered with paper "grass," holds the lollipops in place.

Sunshine-colored straws seem to be growing blossoms! Cut flower shapes in different sizes from foamy sheets, plus one green leaf, punch holes in the pieces and stack them on a straw. Write each child's name on the leaf of her straw to keep things straight.

TO DO

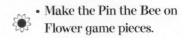

Beforehand

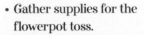

- Make the Pin the Bee on Flower game pieces.
- Gather supplies for the flowerpot toss.
- Make the planters for the swirly pop flowers.
- Fill the piñata.
- Make the flower-topped straws.
- Bake the cupcakes.

Day of

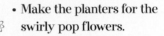

- Make the sandwiches and prepare the veggie "pot."
- Set out the table decorations.
- Mix up the punch.

Fashion a flower stand filled with perennial cupcakes to have out during the party. I stacked several cake plates and covered each with tissue-paper leaves before setting out the blooming cakes.

Supplies

FOR THE INVITATIONS

- Cardstock in a variety of bright colors
- Scissors
- Hole punch
- Paper fastener (brad)
- Markers

FOR THE PARTY

- Yellow tablecloth
- Foamy pails in pink and green
- Play jewelry and other treats
- Green paper "grass"
- Swirl lollipops
- Green Styrofoam blocks
- 4 green foamy sheets
- Construction paper in pink, yellow, orange and green
- Scissors
- Hole punch
- Cake stands
- Green tissue paper
- Flower-shaped piñata
- Treats to fill the piñata

Flower Straws

- Foamy sheets in orange, yellow, bright green and pink
- Scissors
- Hole punch
- Straws in bright garden colors

garden party

Party Time

Little gardeners will love the flower-themed food and games. With all the food cut into flower shapes, it will be as if they picked their whole meal! And drinks that come out of a watering can (a new and clean one, of course!) are unexpected and fun.

Cupcakes are only part of the festivities, as a big flower piñata full of candy sends them home with treats for later. Piñatas can be found at party supply stores—but don't forget you have to buy the goodies to fill them! Don't limit yourself to only candy, either: Stickers, temporary tattoos and hair clips are all great choices, too. Be careful picking anything too large or too heavy, because it will fly out of the piñata and could be dangerous!

Playing Pin the Bee on the Flower is a delightful change from Pin the Tail on the Donkey, and the fun can go on for a long time. Keep them busy with the Flowerpot Toss, and they'll surely be ready for snacks when it's time to sing "Happy Birthday!"

Game Time

These games are both ideal for playing more than once!

FLOWERPOT TOSS

YOU'LL NEED: Two 8-inch flower-pots; 6 bean bags; small prizes

Simple to put together, this game will entertain your little petunias happily!

Divide the children into two teams and line them up in two rows. Place the flowerpots on a flat surface (lawn, patio, or floor) about 3 yards from the kids. Each player gets three chances to toss the bean bags into her team's pot. Every bean bag that lands in the pot is a point for that team—an adult should keep score. Take the bean bags out and hand them to the next player, who gets to try it out herself. After everyone has a turn, the team with the most points wins! Play this game more than once— the best of three games—so everyone has multiple chances to sink a shot.

garden party

PIN THE BEE ON THE FLOWER

YOU'LL NEED: ½ yard pink or white felt (for backing); ½ yard each pink, yellow, orange, purple, brown and green felt; 1 sheet white felt (for flower center); thin wooden dowel 1 yard long; multicolored pom-poms; googly eyes; black chenille stem; pencil; markers; craft glue; scissors; spray adhesive; blindfold

Little Blossoms will be enchanted with this version of Pin the Tail on the Donkey. Whoever places the bee closest to the center of the flower wins!

The backing is made from the large piece of felt. Wrap one edge around the dowel and glue in place, then let dry. In the meantime, cut petals from the colored felt (photocopy the template at the front of the book and use it to trace the shape onto the felt). Trace the flowerpot template onto the brown felt and the stem and leaves on the green. Cut a 6-inch circle from the small white felt square. Glue all the flower pieces onto the front of the backdrop as pictured.

Make the bee out of the remaining yellow felt, using the template at the front of the book as a guide. Embellish the bee with strips of black felt, pom-poms and the chenille stem.

Blindfold each little girl in turn and spin her around a few times. Stand her facing the flower, hand her the bee, and let her walk to the flower and place the bee on it. Once she's done, remove the blindfold and see how close she came! Place a "marker" where she placed the bee so that her spot can be compared with the others: Cut a small leaf shape out of green felt and write her name on it. Press it to the flower, then blindfold the next partier and see how close she gets! Give a prize to the winner.

46

garden party

BUDDING SANDWICHES

These are otherwise straightforward sandwiches—favorites like peanut butter and jelly, cream cheese and jelly, and tuna salad—made infinitely more fun because they are cut into shapes!

Peanut butter
Jelly or jam
Cream cheese
Tuna salad
Whole-grain bread

Make a variety of sandwiches. Using a large flower-shaped cookie cutter, cut a flower out of each sandwich. Make enough for two flower sandwiches per child, and set them out on a platter to add to the decor.

WATERING-CAN PUNCH

32 ounces cranberry-raspberry juice
2 liters sparkling water
4 cups ice cubes

Mix ingredients in a new, unused watering can. Allow each child to hold her cup with a flower straw, and pour her drink for her!

Garden Party Menu
Budding Sandwiches
Pots of Crudités
Watering-Can Punch
Blossoming Cupcakes

POTS OF CRUDITÉS

Carrots, peeled
Celery stalks
Cucumbers, peeled
Red, yellow and orange peppers
Green beans
Small tomatoes, such as cherry
½ cup lowfat sour cream
1 cup nonfat plain yogurt
2 teaspoons dried dill
1 teaspoon dried tarragon
1 teaspoon dried parsley flakes
1 teaspoon paprika

Rinse and dry all the veggies, then cut the carrots, celery, cucumbers and peppers into strips. Trim green beans but leave whole. Line the bottom of a new, unused garden pot with plastic wrap. Stand the veggies in so they look as if they are growing out of the pot. Combine the sour cream through paprika in a bowl and serve alongside.

BLOSSOMING CUPCAKES

Flower cupcakes are perennial. Set them out on a pretty cake stand and these treats are sure to be picked!

Vanilla cupcakes (recipe on page 140)
Vanilla frosting (recipe on page 140)
Food coloring in red, yellow, purple and green
M&M's

Bake the cupcakes according to the directions on page 140. Let cool completely.

  Make a batch of vanilla frosting following the directions on page 140. With a flat knife or offset spatula, frost the cupcakes with white vanilla frosting (leave some plain if you want to reduce the amount of sugar in a portion). Divide the remaining frosting up in four bowls and dye them pink (1 drop red food coloring), yellow (1 drop yellow food coloring), lavender (1 drop purple food coloring) and green (1 drop green food coloring). Fill 4 pastry bags fitted with decorative tips with each of the colored frostings and pipe flowers onto the top of each cupcake. Set an M&M down in the center for the finishing touch.

olympic games ∞

friendly competition

This active party is best held outdoors where there's lots of room for the events. As the excited children play the games, remind them that although the nature of Olympics is competition, it's all in good fun to cheer each other on!

51

olympic games

PARTY TIME!

Duration:
2 hours (11 a.m.–1 p.m.)

11:00–11:30	Races
11:30–12:00	Obstacle Race
12:00–12:30	Lunch
12:30–1:00	Bean Bag Toss and cookies

The Invitations

The Olympic Games date back to ancient times. The modern games use five interlocked rings to represent the different continents coming together in sport, and even the youngest sports fans recognize the image. Colorful rings drawn with markers on white cardstock instantly say "Let the games begin!" Use the bottom of a cup or other round household item to trace the circles, and use markers in the Olympic colors of red, yellow, blue, green and black.

Setting the Scene

This is an active party, so decorations aren't the main focus. Games of this size require a big open space to be played. If the party is being held indoors, be sure to clear enough room for the activities.

To give the space a special feel, we took large wooden circles, found in the floral section of the crafts store, painted them with acrylic paint and glued them together to mimic the Olympic symbol. We hung it on an ivy wall, making it an ideal backdrop for the competition. You could hang it off your porch or on the side of the house.

Uniforms are a must for every athlete! Once you know the guest list, buy T-shirts in each child's native country's team color, then stencil the official Olympic country code (look them up online) using fabric paint or iron-on letters. Add a number for competition using fabric paints or iron-on numbers.

TO DO

Beforehand

- Purchase T-shirts in a variety of colors to fit the kids.
- Stencil the T-shirts.
- Paint the Olympic rings.
- Gather the game items, such as the potato sacks and bean bags.
- Bake and decorate the Medal Cookies.
- Prepare the frozen yogurt pops.

Day of

- Print and cover the water bottles.
- Decorate the table.
- Plan obstacles for the obstacle race.
- Bake the Sausage Rolls.
- Mix up the punch.

Supplies

FOR THE INVITATIONS
- White cardstock
- Markers in red, yellow, blue, green and black

FOR THE PARTY
- 5 wooden circles (from a crafts or garden store)
- Acrylic paint in red, yellow, blue, green and black
- Paintbrushes
- Glue
- Tape
- Mini country flags
- Styrofoam half-sphere
- Tissue paper in red
- Glue sticks

Uniforms
- T-shirts in various colors to fit the party-goers
- Letter and number stencils and black fabric paint OR iron-on letters and numbers

Water Bottles
- 8 plastic water bottles
- White copy paper
- Computer and printer

olympic games

Party Time

Athletes can make a quick pit stop at the water table to pick up their water bottle to keep hydrated. Labels designed on the computer and printed out are affixed with double-sided tape. The water station doubles as a snack table and houses the display of medal cookies and awards. We covered the table with a green tablecloth and made a little display for flags of the nations. We covered a half-sphere of Styrofoam with red tissue paper and stuck the purchased flags into it.

The games are varied and simple but provide lots of active enjoyment. Bean Bag Toss, Three-Legged Race and Sack Races get the children moving around and burning off energy. Play whistles give them authority and add to the playfulness. Sacks for races are from a party store; cones and bean bags found were at a toy store. Gold Medal Cookies are the just reward for all the playtime.

Game Time

SACK RACES

YOU'LL NEED: Potato sacks or pillowcases; a cone; prizes

Potato sack races are an age-old tradition. Nowadays you can find sacks in mail-order catalogs or on the Internet. Pillowcases can work just as well, if you have them to spare!

Divide the children into two teams. Line them up behind one another and give the first child a sack. Place two cones about 6 yards from each team. On the starter's call of "On your mark, get set, go!" the first player hops in the sack to the cone and back, handing off the sack to the next in line. The team that finishes first wins!

THREE-LEGGED RACE

YOU'LL NEED: Scarf or ribbon; small prizes such as medals

Pair the kids up and have them stand side by side. Tie their touching legs together with a scarf or ribbon. Line all the pairs up at one end of the yard and establish a finish line on the other side. The first team across wins!

OBSTACLE COURSE

YOU'LL NEED: Various objects that can be used as "obstacles"; small prizes

Get creative with this one! Set up start and finish lines on opposite ends of the yard, and in between place various obstacles that have to be performed before kids can cross the finish line. Some ideas include a small carton to jump over; a hoop for hula hooping 4 or 5 rounds; an inflatable tube to slip down the body; a spot for doing 3 jumping jacks. Divide the children into two teams; the team to complete the course first wins.

BEAN BAG TOSS

YOU'LL NEED: 3 bean bags per kid; 1 bucket

Line the children up and give each 3 bean bags. Place a bucket about 3 yards away from them. On the starter's call of "On your mark, get set, go!" the children toss the bean bags into the bucket. This is a fun game with no winner declared. The game ends after each child gets several tosses.

olympic games

SAUSAGE ROLLS

2 pounds sausage meat, casings removed
2 cups shredded mozzarella cheese
1 fresh or frozen pizza dough

Preheat the oven to 425°F. In a bowl, mix together the sausage and cheese. On a lightly floured surface, roll out the dough to ¼-inch thickness. Cut the dough into 3-inch-square pieces. Place a heaping spoonful of the sausage mixture in the middle of each square and roll the dough around the filling. Place on a cookie sheet and bake for 20 minutes or until golden brown.

FROZEN YOGURT POPS

Use fruits of your choosing. For a non-dairy treat substitute juice for the yogurt.

1 16-ounce bag frozen mixed berries
6 6-ounce containers vanilla yogurt

Pour the frozen berries in a bowl and let stand for 10–15 minutes at room temperature, or until juices start to run. Add the yogurt and mix well. Scoop the mixture into popsicle molds according to the manufacturer's directions. Freeze overnight.

Athlete's Menu
Sausage Rolls
Podium Punch
Frozen Yogurt Pops
Medal Cookies

MEDAL COOKIES

1½ cups all-purpose flour
1 teaspoon baking powder
¼ teaspoon salt
½ cup unsalted butter
¾ cup sugar
1 large egg
1 teaspoon vanilla extract
Decorative icing in white, red, green, blue, yellow and black
Gold icing glaze
Star-shaped sugar sprinkles

In a medium bowl, sift together the flour, baking powder and salt. In a large bowl using a handheld mixer, beat together the butter and sugar until light and fluffy. Add the egg and vanilla and beat until creamy. With the mixer on low, slowly add the flour mixture.

Gather the dough into a ball, cover it in plastic wrap and let chill for at least one hour until ready to use.

Preheat oven to 350°F. Divide the dough into thirds and remove one third; keep the remaining dough in the fridge until ready to use. On a lightly floured surface, roll the dough out to about ¼-inch thick. Using a 4-inch circle cookie cutter, cut out the cookies and transfer to baking sheets. Repeat until the remaining dough is used.

Bake the cookies for 10–12 minutes, or until light brown. Let cool before decorating.

Frost the cookies lightly with white icing. Pipe decorative icing around the outer edges of the cookies in a variety of Olympic ring colors. Squeeze gold icing glaze in the centers. Sprinkle with star confections. Place cookies on platter to allow icing to set.

PODIUM PUNCH

32 ounces lemonade
8 ounces frozen raspberries in juice, defrosted
2 liters lemon-flavored seltzer
4 cups ice cubes

In a larger pitcher mix the lemonade and frozen raspberries. Top with seltzer and serve over ice.

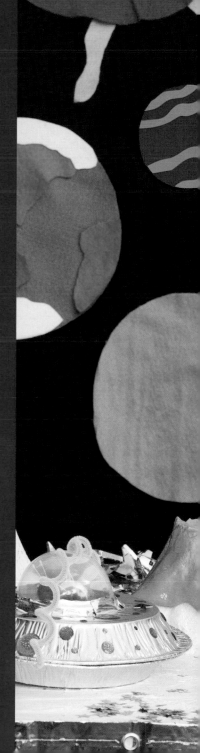

out·of·the·world

outer space adventure!

Preschoolers are often fascinated by the immense size of the universe and all that it holds. This is a wonderful party to celebrate their curiosity—with a rocket ship, lots of stars, planets and out-of-this-world crafts.

outer space adventure!

SCHEDULE

Duration:
Approximately 2 hours
(10 a.m.–12 p.m.)

10:00–10:30	Make flying saucers
10:30–11:00	Games
11:00–11:30	Play in rocket ship
11:30-12:00	Lunch and cake

Invitations

Rocket ships cut from brightly colored paper in red, blue or white are easy to make and so much fun! Draw a rocket ship and cut it out. You and your child can add shiny star stickers and use glitter markers to decorate a basic rocket shape. Sprinkle a bit of starry confetti in the envelope for a solar surprise. Important details can be mentioned in the invitation in a fun way: Blast Off! (date and start time), Landing (end time), Mission Control (address) and Reply to Mission Commander (RSVP details).

Setting the Scene

The decorations for this party require more time than some others, so that materials and paint can dry fully. Be sure to start the decorations days before the party so that everything is ready in time!

We held this party outdoors when it was warm, but it is easily held inside. If you're having it indoors, take the time to craft planets and stars out of cardboard before the party (see templates at the front of the book). Paint the planets in various colors and cover the stars with silver glitter. Hang the stars and planets from fishing line over the party space—they'll seem to float overhead! Go one step further by covering the other walls with black crepe paper and silver glitter stars—add white twinkle lights to complete the starry scene. Clear the room for the rocket ship and to make room for games. Outdoors, we made a simple planet backdrop out of a length of black felt. We cut circles and stars out of colored felt to make the planets. The felt sticks to felt, but if your planets are falling

TO DO

Beforehand

- Make the tablescape and rocket ship.
- Prep the flying saucers.
- Make cardboard planets for hanging and hiding.
- Bake the cake.

Day of

- Make the Moon Rover for candy.
- Prepare the T-shirts.
- Blow up the balloons.
- Cut the Fruit Kabobs.
- Cook the sliders and mix up the punch.

Supplies

FOR THE INVITATIONS
- Red, blue and white construction paper
- Scissors
- Star stickers
- Glitter markers
- Confetti

FOR THE PARTY
- Cardboard
- Paint in various colors
- Glitter
- Black crepe paper
- Twinkle lights
- Sheet of black felt
- Colored felt
- Tape

Lunar Tablescape
- 1 30-by-48-inch plywood board
- 5 plastic flowerpots, 6 and 8 inches wide
- Cheesecloth
- 2 4-pound tubs plaster of Paris dry mix
- Plastic drop cloths
- Neon-colored play dough

Lunar Candy Rover
- Empty shoebox
- 4 mini pie tins
- Neon or brightly colored pom-poms, stickers and chenille stems

Rocket Ship
- 1 wardrobe box
- 1 medium-sized box
- 1 roll heavy aluminum foil
- 2 cans white spray paint, flat finish
- Red and silver duct tape
- Adhesive-backed foam sheets with glitter finish in red and blue
- Reflective number and arrow stickers

Flying Saucers
- 10 foil pie tins
- 10 clear plastic drink cup tops (like for a frozen drink at a coffee shop)
- Mini adhesive pom-pom Martians

outer space adventure!

down, use some tape to keep them in place.

The tablescape, resembling a lunar site, might look complicated, but it is rather easy to make. It is very messy, though, so be sure to protect your work area indoors with plastic drop cloths, or make it outside. The plywood piece will serve as the base. Arrange the plastic flowerpots right side up on the base, and drape with cheesecloth. Follow the package directions for the plaster of Paris to mix it with enough water to make a yogurt-like consistency, and pour the mixture over the cheesecloth until the entire surface is covered. The weight of the plaster will gently cave in the cheesecloth at the opening of the pots; this will look just like craters when dry! Let set fully before painting the table and craters various colors. Allow to dry completely. Decorate the lunar surface with little Martian men, glittery stars and streamers.

Sitting on the lunar surface tablescape is, of course, a Moon Rover! Ours is filled with treats for the hungry astronauts. To make the Rover, cover a large shoebox with aluminum foil. Staple or glue mini pie tins to the sides to resemble wheels, and decorate the whole Rover with stickers, chenille stems and pom-poms. Fill the box with an assortment of candy and treats that are free for the taking.

Not just decor, the rocket ship is an eye-catching centerpiece that will keep little space pioneers playing for hours—they can pretend to go to the moon in it! Ours was made from cardboard boxes picked up from a local moving company: a large wardrobe box for the body and a medium-size box cut into a point at the top. Use a tall wardrobe box as the base. With a sharp knife, cut off the flaps and cut a door and windows into the sides. Spray the entire base with white spray paint and let dry fully (this may take an entire day, so plan enough time). Once it is dry, decorate it with red and blue stickers and paint. Make the pointed top by cutting the four sides of the medium box into triangles, then lean the triangles against each other and tape them into place. Cover the top with heavy-duty aluminum foil, decorate it with stars and place it atop the base. Secure it with duct tape on the inside if necessary.

Flying saucers are easy to decorate and fun to play with. Beforehand, staple two aluminum pie tins with right sides together. Place a Martian (found at crafts stores) on top and cover with a plastic lid. Set out stickers and chenille stems in bright colors and allow the kids to decorate their saucers. Let them throw the saucers around the party as they go on space adventures!

outer space adventure!

Party Time

As our astronauts are little ones, we embellished plain white T-shirts with silver duct tape and glittery stars in red and blue to help them feel the part. When they arrive at the party, each kid gets a shirt to put on. The stars are cut from adhesive-backed glitter foam sheets. Wrap each sleeve with a band of silver duct tape and add small stars on top, then place a strip of tape with blue and red stars at the breast pocket. Everyone gets to wear their "spacesuit" at the party and can take it with them for playing astronaut at home!

Games and playing with the rocket ship keep kids occupied until it's time for cake!

Game Time

FLYING SAUCERS

YOU'LL NEED: Hula hoop; flying saucers; small prizes

Place the hula hoop about 6 feet away and organize the kids into a line. One at a time, each tries to toss his or her flying saucer into the ring. Misses sit out until the next round; those who land their saucer in the ring get to go again. With each round, move the line back 1 foot to increase the difficulty. When only one saucer lands in the hoop, that astronaut is the winner!

FIND THE PLANETS

YOU'LL NEED: Small painted cardboard planets and stars (made ahead of time); small prizes

Children love a scavenger hunt, and this is just another version of the classic game. Hide the planets and stars in the garden or around the party room if the party is indoors. The found planets and stars can then be exchanged for prizes!

BALLOON POP RACE

YOU'LL NEED: 2 cardboard boxes, one for each team, with the tops and bottoms cut off, decorated like spaceships (wrap in foil and decorate like the rocket ship); balloons (enough for all the children and a few extra); 2 large trash bags

This was so popular at the last party that I had to blow up more balloons to play it a second time!

Place the balloons in the trash bags (keep bags open so they act as a container) and set them about 10 yards away from each box. Divide the children into two teams and line them up behind each box. Say, "On your mark, get set, go!" and the first child in each team hops in a box, picks it up around herself, runs to where the balloons are, takes a balloon, sits on it to pop it, and then runs, in the box, back to her team. The next child hops in the box as the first one hops out and gets a turn. Whichever team finishes first wins!

outer space adventure!

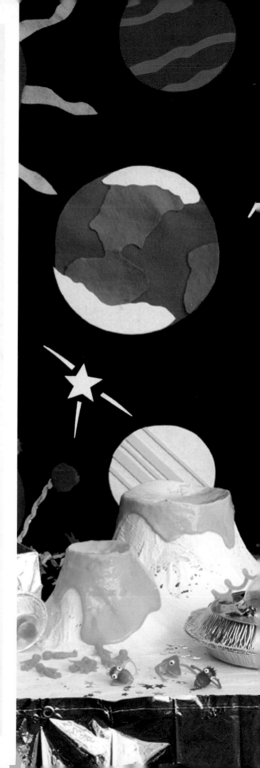

SPACE SLIDERS

These mini turkey burgers are a real favorite with little ones, and they're healthier than a beef burger.

2   pounds ground turkey
1   egg
½ cup bread crumbs
½ cup chopped tomatoes
¼ cup shredded carrots
2   tablespoons tomato sauce
18 mini buns
Lettuce leaves
Ketchup, mustard and
      other condiments

Mix the turkey through the tomato sauce in a large bowl. Scoop about ⅓ cup of the mixture and form into a small patty about 3 inches in diameter. Repeat with remaining mixture; you should have about 18 patties. Heat a grill pan over medium heat and cook the patties until browned, about 6 minutes each side. Serve with the buns, lettuce and condiments.

Outer Space Menu
Space Sliders
Martian Punch
Rocket Ship Cake
Starry Fruit Kabobs

MARTIAN PUNCH

48 ounces grape juice
24 ounces lime-flavored seltzer
1   bottle green maraschino cherries
4   cups ice

Mix all ingredients in a plastic pitcher. Serve in silver plastic cups with bright green straws.

STARRY FRUIT KABOBS

1   honeydew melon
1   cantaloupe
1   small watermelon
1   pineapple
4   apples
6   bananas
12 wooden skewers

Cut all fruit except bananas lengthwise into ½-inch slices. Using a 1-inch metal star cookie cutter, cut the fruit into star shapes. Slice the bananas into 2-inch pieces. Arrange the fruit on the wooden skewers.

outer space adventure!

ROCKET SHIP CAKE

- 1 box of cake mix or recipe on page 140 or 141, flavor of choice
- 1½ cans vanilla frosting or recipe on page 140
- Fondant in blue, red and yellow
- Black food coloring
- 1 wafer ice cream cone
- 6 spice drops, 2 each yellow, red and orange
- M&M's candies in gray
- Silver sprinkles

Bake the cake in a 9-by-13-inch pan following package directions, or use recipe on page 140 or 141. Let cool. Remove from pan onto a flat, clean surface. With a knife, cut an oval shape for the rocket body and two side launchers out of the flat cake. Place the rocket body on a serving platter or board and set the side launcher pieces in place according to the photo. Use vanilla frosting to "glue" the launchers to the body, and cover the whole cake with frosting. On a cutting board or work surface, with a rolling pin, roll the red, yellow and blue fondant into sheets. Cut strips and door shape as desired, using the photo as a guide. Lay these pieces onto the cake along with M&M's for rivets. To make the fuselage, cut the top off of the wafer cone so you have a ring, then coat it with icing inside and out and cover it with silver sprinkles. Push it gently into the back of cake. With a rolling pin, flatten spice drops and layer them into the rocket base as flames.

ALL ABOUT FONDANT

- Fondant, a sweet, sugary paste, is most often used to form a perfectly smooth coating for cakes and confections. It offers a fresh canvas to decorate on, and at the same time acts as a sealant to lock the freshness in.

- Found in many colors, fondant is sold in thick blocks and must be rolled into a smooth, pliable state. It can be rolled into a sheet to cover a cake for a neat, smooth finish, or rolled and cut into strips or shapes depending on what the theme of the cake or dessert may be. The color can be further altered by kneading in a few drops of food coloring.

Working with Fondant:

- Sprinkle a countertop or smooth surface with sifted confectioners' sugar. Roll out the fondant to a thickness of about ¼ inch using a confectioners' sugar-dusted rolling pin. Sifted sugar is important: any lumps will leave pit marks in the fondant.

- Spread a thin layer of regular frosting over the cake. Lay the fondant over the frosting, smoothing out the surface and working your way down the sides. An icing spreader or flat edge of a knife works well to help smooth and tuck corners. Trim any excess off the bottom and sides. Decorate the fondant surface as desired.

- For shapes and decorative accessories, use a knife or cookie cutter to cut and shape the fondant. Brush a tiny bit of water over the base of the decoration so that it adheres to the cake.

merry mermaids

sea princesses

A mermaid's mystical world is a magical place, where everything seems to glisten and float about. Take cues from the turquoise and blue colors of the ocean and bright greens of the seaweed to re-create this world on land. A mermaid party is also a fun idea for winter birthday girls who miss out on pool parties in the warmer months, as it can easily be held indoors. Just be sure the party space is warm and the mermaids have their legs covered, and watch the daughters of Triton make a splash!

sea princesses

SCHEDULE

Duration:
Approximately 2 hours
(11 a.m. – 1 p.m.)

11:00–11:30	Dress-up
11:30–12:00	Crown decorating and games
12:00–12:30	Lunch and cake
12:30–1:00	Games

Invitations

Sparkly under-the-sea invites are a must for this party! Iridescent cardstock comes in a variety of colors, or create the effect yourself using glittery pens on regular paper. From a folded piece of cardstock, cut a shell or starfish shape, keeping one folded side attached. Lift it open and write all of the party information inside, with an opening message such as "King Triton has requested your presence at Jenny's birthday…" or "Calling all mermaids to celebrate" or "Dive in and help make Sarah's birthday a splash!"

Setting the Scene

Go "under the sea" in this special watery "cave"! Hang a hula hoop from the ceiling and attach tulle, ribbons and crepe paper streamers from it to create a mermaid-only haven. If you're outside or the windows are open, the streamers will flutter in the breeze and appear to be floating in the water.

The treasure-filled tablescape starts with a plastic purple cloth with a purple tulle overlay. The tulle is bunched at points to create the illusion of waves to fit with the frothy, mystical look elsewhere in the room. Our centerpiece, a candelabra, was made by adhering homemade play dough, tinted light blue, to an old candle holder, and then pushing painted shells, pearls, gems and sequins into the wet dough. To make the play dough, combine the flour, salt, water and cooking oil until smooth.

Add a few drops of food coloring, until the color is as desired. After covering the candlestick holder, let it dry overnight.

Set the finished candelabra on a silver platter and pile the base with gumballs in sea tones, pearl necklaces and glistening candies. Treasure boxes— purchased foamy boxes that you can glue shells and beads to—hold more goodies, including candy necklaces and bracelets to adorn the fishtailed crowd.

Shells make the perfect place cards when painted in a glittery finish with each mermaid's name. Next time you're at the beach, collect large clamshells for this party! (Or you can always find them for sale at crafts stores.) Coat them with glitter glue, then write names with a glitter pen. Each mermaid can take her shell home to use as a paperweight!

Supplies

FOR THE INVITATIONS

- Iridescent cardstock
- Scissors
- Markers

FOR THE PARTY

Candelabra

- 1 candle holder
- 1 cup all-purpose flour
- ½ cup salt
- ½ cup water
- 2 teaspoons cooking oil
- Blue food coloring
- Assorted shells, gems and pearl notions
- Silver platter
- Gumballs, candy necklaces and other treats
- Large shells
- Glitter paint in clear finish
- Pink acrylic paint
- Paintbrushes
- Foamy boxes in blue and green
- 3 yards white sequin trim
- Assorted pearl notions

Costumes

- 10 white tank tops
- 1 tube fabric paint in turquoise glitter finish
- 5 yards turquoise sequin fabric
- 5 yards bright blue sequin fabric
- White yarn
- Blue ribbon
- Headbands
- Glue
- 10 large white foamy sheets
- Glitter glue in green and blue
- Assorted gems and sequins

Hula hoop

- 5 rolls crepe paper streamers in purple, light green, bright green, light blue and bright blue
- 10 yards ½-inch-wide grosgrain ribbon
- 6 yards light green tulle
- 4 yards lavender tulle
- Fishing line
- Tape

sea princesses

DO IT

Beforehand

- Craft the mermaid cave.
- Make the play dough and create the centerpiece.
- Decorate the treasure boxes.
- Make the crowns.
- Prepare the skirts and wigs.

Day of

- Bake the Madeleines and prepare the rest of the food.
- Set the tablescape.
- Set out cups and skewers for sodas.

Party Time

Transforming from a little girl into a mermaid makes this party an escape! Provide materials for making costumes, crowns and even long wigs, and the girls can truly be little mermaids.

Costumes are relatively easy to prepare, actually. We asked everyone to wear pastel-colored leggings, and then we provided the tops and bottoms that they could change into if they wanted. I bought white tank tops at a large discount store and stenciled glittery starfish on them (use the template at the back of the book). They doubled as very fashionable favors! The shimmery skirts are pieces of fabric. We bunched up extra length and fastened it with a safety pin to form a tail and to shape the legs. The girls simply knotted the fabric at the waist to fit.

Wigs of seaworthy tresses get little ones even more in the mood. Strands of white yarn and lengths of ribbon are secured to a headband and allowed to flow down her shoulders.

Decorating crowns—the original Little Mermaid was a princess, after all—keeps the girls busy between games and snacks. I formed the bases ahead of time by cutting a foamy sheet into fun seaweed-like spikes and gluing the ends together. Then I provided ribbons, jewels and gems to be glued on for a personal touch. The crowns can dry while games are played!

Game Time

PIN THE PEARL IN THE OYSTER

YOU'LL NEED: One 24-by-36-inch sheet poster board; gray and black poster paint; marker; 2 white foamy sheets with pearlized finish; double-sided tape; blindfold; small prizes

Draw a large oyster shape on the poster board and cut it out. With gray paint, color the oyster. Draw a star where the pearl should be placed—at the center of the open oyster is best. Hang the oyster on the wall. Cut the foamy sheets into round pearls about 2 inches in diameter each.

Write each child's name on a pearl and adhere a length of double-sided tape to the back. The first kid to go should be blindfolded and spun around a few times. Aim her at the oyster and let her walk up and stick her pearl to the oyster. See how close she got! After everyone has a chance to go, see who placed her pearl the closest to the designated spot: She wins!

SNATCH

YOU'LL NEED: Assortment of ocean-themed objects

This is a fun game of memory and guessing.

Clear the party table and place several objects in the center. It's fun to make sure they're related to the theme of the party: a shell bracelet, plastic fish, a glimmery shell. Hide them with a tablecloth or keep the partiers in a different area of the room until you're ready. Set a timer for 15 seconds and designate one girl as the guesser for the round. Secretly designate one of the remaining girls as the stealer and reveal the table to all. Give the kids 15 seconds to look at the items, then have the guesser turn her back as the stealer snatches one item and hides it in her lap. The guesser then turns around and tries to recall what item was taken away, and guesses who did it. Allow a few guesses, then have the snatcher reveal herself and return the item to the table. Rearrange the objects and even swap out a few for new ones. The snatcher then is the guesser for the next round; once she turns her back, point to the next person to steal. Play continues until everyone has had a chance to snatch and guess.

MERMAID'S TREASURE

YOU'LL NEED: Assortment of everyday objects (not ocean-themed); small prizes

In the movie *The Little Mermaid*, Ariel is fascinated by the objects from the "other world" (above the sea), so with that in mind, I created this scavenger hunt. Before the party, hide items from the "other world" such as a hand mirror, fork, spoon, hanger, toothbrush, etc., around the party space. (Keep a list so that you'll know when everything has been located.) Have the mermaids work together to find them all for Ariel! Give small prizes such as stickers or hair clips to the girls who find the objects.

sea princesses

TURKEY AND TUNA SALAD WRAPS

With an option for either tuna or turkey, there's a sandwich to suit everyone's taste!

Ranch dressing
10 whole wheat, spinach or tomato tortillas
1 cup shredded lettuce
1 cup shredded carrots
1 pound tuna salad
1 pound sliced fresh turkey breast

Spread approximately 1 teaspoon of ranch dressing on a tortilla. Toward one edge, sprinkle a bit of lettuce, then carrots, and add a small scoop of tuna salad or a piece of turkey breast. Roll the tortilla up, cut in half and secure with toothpicks. Repeat with the remaining tortillas.

MERMAID PURSE PIES

4 6-ounce containers blueberry yogurt
1 6-ounce container whipped topping
12 mini piecrusts in foil tins
Fresh blueberries, for garnish

In a mixing bowl, combine the yogurt and whipped topping. Spoon the mixture into the pie tins and top with blueberries. Chill until ready to serve.

Mermaid Menu
Turkey and Tuna Salad Wraps
Sea Pearl Salad
Mermaid Purse Pies
Sea Urchin Sodas
Shimmery Shell Cakes

SEA PEARL SALAD

As enticing as shiny pearls found in oysters, but much more delicious!

1 honeydew melon
1 cantaloupe
Half a seedless watermelon

Cut the honeydew and cantaloupe in half and scoop out the seeds. Using a melon baller, scoop the flesh of both melons and the watermelon into small balls. Mix them all up in a bowl and serve.

SEA URCHIN SODAS

6 16-ounce bottles white grape soda
White grapes on skewers, for garnish

The grapes look like pearls and make a festive and fancy garnish in the soda!

SHIMMERY SHELL CAKES

These mini cakes—actually Madeleine cookies—are a tasty alternative to traditional birthday cake. Set them out on a pretty cake stand with large pearl gumballs in the center.

1 batch vanilla cake (see recipe on page 140)
1 batch vanilla frosting (see recipe on page 140)
Food coloring in green and purple, or blue and red.
Pearl confections

Prepare the batter for the vanilla cake as directed on page 140. Pour into Madeleine molds and bake 14–18 minutes or until light golden brown. Let cool before removing from pan. Prepare the vanilla frosting as directed on page 140 and dye half of it with a drop or two of green and in a separate bowl, dye the other half with a drop or two of purple (or a mixture of blue and red) food coloring. Frost halves of the Madeleines, from the tips halfway down. Sprinkle with pearl confections.

take me out to the ballgame!

batter up!

A party centered around America's favorite pastime is sure to be a hit with the younger crowd. A festive setting, energetic games and sweet treats are sure to send your party guests home swinging—in a good way, of course!

ballgame!

SCHEDULE

Duration:
Approximately 2 hours
(10 a.m.–12 p.m.)

10:00–10:30	Make pennants
10:30–11:00	Batting practice
11:00–11:30	Games
11:30–12:00	Lunch and cake

Invitations

A card made to look like a baseball will have the invitees geared up and ready to play. A 4-inch diameter circle cut from crisp white cardstock is the base, and red marker is used to form the lacing. Use the center for a greeting such as "Batter Up!" or "Get Swinging," and on the back list all of the party details. Clever names for all the info set the mood: Instead of the location, note the "Ballpark," and instead of the start time, give the hour of the "Opening Pitch."

Setting the Scene

Pennant flags hanging about evoke a baseball field of dreams. Make colorful generic pennants or gather pennants from specific teams. Groups of bright red and blue balloons are tied in bunches and placed around the field. Bases are set up for the big game—ours were from a sports store, but they can easily be crafted from white felt or foamy sheets.

Party Time

Have the players arrive in their favorite team's jersey and hat. Start the warm-up by having the kids decorate their own baseball pennants with festive stickers and their name in glitter pen.

When all the players are in the stadium, the game or games can begin! Having all the children get a chance at batting practice is a fun warm-up, and at this age a formal game can be daunting and a little too ambitious. Rough-and-tumble boys will like being able to run around and expend some energy.

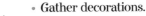

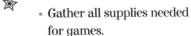

TO DO

Beforehand

- Gather decorations.
- Gather all supplies needed for games.
- Make Baseball Pops.

Day of

- Make meatballs and slaw.

A soft bat and Wiffle or spongey balls make for safe play no matter how the balls might land! Easy games like a Spoon-and-Egg Run of the bases, Hide-and-Seek with Baseball Cards, and a game of Baseball Balloons keep things light and playful.

An athlete's menu will assure energy and stamina for the duration of the party. Cake pops finish the game and are a unique way to have a ball of a birthday cake!

Supplies

FOR THE INVITATIONS
- White cardstock
- Red marker

FOR THE PARTY
- Team pennants
- Balloons in blue and red
- Ribbon
- Baseball bases (from a sporting goods store) or white foamy sheets
- Foamy pennants
- Baseball-themed stickers
- Glitter pens
- Permanent marker
- Nerf bat
- Wiffle or spongey balls

ballgame!

Game Time

Baseball minded games geared for little players yield fun for all.

SPOON-AND-EGG RUNNING OF THE BASES

YOU'LL NEED: 4 hard-boiled eggs; 2 large spoons; small prizes

This is a game where all children are on the same team, and it's a test of balance and concentration that might just be disrupted by the other children's egging each other on!

Line the children up at home plate and give the first child an egg set in the spoon. Taking turns, have the children go one by one around the bases, balancing the egg. If they drop their egg, they are "out." If they make it around all the bases with the egg on the spoon, they go to the back of the line in order to go again! Last one who hasn't dropped an egg is the winner.

BASEBALL BALLOONS

YOU'LL NEED: Balloons; small prizes

The object of Baseball Balloons is to keep the balloon floating for as long as possible. Divide the children into two teams and give each team one blown-up balloon. Pitch the balloons into the air at the same time, and see how long the teams can keep the balloon aloft! When a balloon hits the floor, stop the play and start over again!

BATTING PRACTICE

YOU'LL NEED: Bat; ball

Designate one kid—or an adult—as the pitcher, and set up one batter at home plate. Everyone else is in the outfield. A gentle pitch to the batter, a swing, and if contact is made, the kid who catches the ball gets to be the batter next! Step in to ensure that all the kids get a chance at bat, and give each batter plenty of tries to get a hit.

HIDE-AND-SEEK BASEBALL CARDS

YOU'LL NEED: Packages of baseball cards

This game is more of a treasure hunt than hide-and-seek. Hide wrapped packages of baseball cards around the party space (make notes for yourself so you know where everything is!). Monitor the play, guiding kids who are "hot" or "cold" if necessary, to be sure everyone gets a pack or two. Baseballs, packages of stickers or small plastic hats filled with candy are other great items to hide.

ballgame!

SLIDER SLAW

Kids love this coleslaw and eat it by the ton! The apple and mango give the cabbage a perfect sweet-and-sour kick.

1 medium head green cabbage, shredded
½ head red cabbage, shredded
2 large carrots, shredded
1 Granny Smith apple, core removed, cut into small chunks
1 ripe mango, peeled and cut into small chunks
¼ cup buttermilk
½ cup mayonnaise
3 tablespoons sugar
2 tablespoons vinegar
½ teaspoon salt

Combine shredded cabbages, carrots, apple, and mango in a bowl. In a separate bowl, whisk together the buttermilk, mayonnaise, sugar, vinegar and salt. Add the buttermilk mixture to the slaw and mix well to combine.

ROOT BEER FLOATS

1 half-gallon vanilla ice cream
3 liters root beer

Place 2 scoops of vanilla ice cream into a cup for each kid. Slowly pour the root beer over the ice cream.

Ballpark Menu
Turkey Meatballs
Slider Slaw
Root Beer Floats
Baseball Pops

TURKEY MEATBALLS

Meatballs are loaded with protein and are easy for little ballplayers to eat.

3 pounds ground turkey
½ cup marinara sauce
½ cup unseasoned breadcrumbs
2 tablespoons olive oil

In a bowl, mix all ingredients together. Shape into 1-inch balls. In a large skillet, heat the olive oil over medium heat. Add the meatballs and cook, turning, until browned and cooked through, about 8 minutes. Remove with a slotted spoon. Skewer the meatballs on bamboo skewers to serve.

BASEBALL POPS

1 chocolate cake (recipe on page 141)
1 batch vanilla frosting (recipe on page 140)
14 ounces white chocolate candy melts or 12 ounces white chocolate morsels
Red decorative icing

Preheat the oven to 350°F. Prepare the cake batter using the recipe on page 141. Butter and lightly flour a 9-by-13-inch baking pan. Pour the batter into the pan and bake 30–35 minutes or until a toothpick comes out clean. Let cool in the pan. Crumble it into a bowl. Add ½ cup of the frosting and mix well. Shape the mixture into 2-inch balls, placing on a baking sheet lined with wax paper.

Melt the white chocolate in a bowl in the microwave according to package directions. Pierce a cake ball with a lollipop stick and dip the cake ball into the melted chocolate, coating well. Set the "pops" in a piece of Styrofoam to stand upright while they set.

When the chocolate coating has solidified, pipe on the red lacing using the red icing.

beary
friends
🐾 picnic
teddy time

A teddy bear picnic is the perfect first party for younger kids. Since their teddy bears are invited to join in the fun, they're not away from their best friend, and that makes the whole experience less daunting.

89

beary friends picnic

SCHEDULE

Duration:
2 hours (10 a.m.–12 p.m.)

10:00–10:30	Face painting
10:30–11:00	Games
11:00–11:30	Lunch and cake
11:30–12:00	Games

Invitations

Bear shapes (see template at the back of the book) cut from brown cardstock are sweet as can be. Cut a lighter brown piece for the belly, adhere it with a glue stick, and write the party details there. Instead of drawing the eyes and face on the bear, you could use buttons as eyes. Be clear on the invite that every kid's own teddy bear is invited, too!

Setting the Scene

For this theme you'll find most of what you need around the house. Teddy bears in all sizes along with their stuffed friends sit merrily in wagons, in small chairs and along the garden path. Frame your party space with bears cut from poster board (use template from the invitations as a guide), who seemingly march gaily to the picnic among the garden flowers. Cut the bears from poster board and layer them with glued-on brown kraft paper and lighter brown construction paper to give them color. Draw eyes and noses on with a black marker, or glue large black buttons on as eyes, and glue to a wooden dowel so they can stand up in the yard. Small bits of colored paper give them some flair. They are joined by oversized brightly colored flowers cut from felt, made by cutting several layers of flower shapes from felt and gluing a few colorful layers to a wooden dowel.

We set out "splat mats" in vibrant colors and patterns so that the kids

TO DO

Beforehand

- Craft the teddy bears and flowers for the garden.

- Build the fishing pond.

- Make a playlist of teddy-bear-themed songs.

- Bake and decorate the cookies.

- Bake the cake.

Day of

- Prepare the sandwiches.

- Slice the veggies and fruit.

- Make the lemonade.

could picnic on the lawn or even indoors without making a mess. A few little chairs and soft pillows make easy landing places for tired partiers. Plastic tea sets and plates of sweet cookies set gaily about keep little people interested and entertained.

Supplies

FOR THE INVITATIONS

- Cardstock in two shades of brown
- Scissors
- Glue stick
- Markers
- Buttons, optional
- Thread, optional
- Needle, optional

FOR THE PARTY

- Stuffed teddy bears, for play
- Small teddy bears, for favors
- Wagons
- Chairs
- Face painting kit
- Bear-themed books, for favors

Paper Bears

- 8 sheets 24-by-36-inch poster board (one sheet per bear)
- Roll of brown kraft paper
- Brown construction paper
- Glue
- Markers
- Assorted buttons
- Origami or printed paper
- Wooden dowels

Felt Flowers

- ½ yard each colored felt in purple, pink, light blue, yellow, orange and green
- Spray adhesive
- Wooden dowels

Bear Ears

- 1 yard felt in two shades of brown
- Headbands
- Brown ribbon
- Glue

beary friends picnic

Party Time

The party guests not only play with their teddy bears at this party, they can become bears who party! Teddy bear noses applied with face paint are cute accents for willing bears. Ears, made from shades of brown felt (see template at the back of the book) are glued to ribbon-wrapped headbands—each child gets a pair to take home.

Once the party has begun, the games begin! Fishing for ducks in a "pond" will get them feeling like bears in the woods—plus there are no winners or losers in this game. Simple games like Teddy Bear Hokey Pokey, dancing to music, and having tea with your bear are less structured but give younger children more freedom to play.

Simple eats are most fitting for this crowd, so I made finger sandwiches cut in bear shapes and provided a lot of finger foods, like apple slices, carrot sticks and orange sections. But there's no forgetting the cake. A polka-dot confection sets a happy tone.

Game Time

FISHING FOR DUCKS

YOU'LL NEED: Blue kraft paper; foamy sheets in various colors; pom-poms; googly eyes; glue; mini rubber ducks; adhesive-backed magnets with north and south orientations; wooden dowels; string

Magnetized fishing poles and magnetic prizes make "fishing" in this pond a sure hit! Build the pond out of blue kraft paper and cut lily pads and flowers out of foamy sheets. Pom-pom caterpillars—the bait!—are medium-sized pompoms glued together and adorned with googly eyes. Small magnetic circles with adhesive backs are stuck on the caterpillars' undersides and on the ducks' bellies—be sure that all the caterpillars and all the ducks have magnets with the opposite attraction (so that the caterpillars will attract the ducks, not repel them). Tie the caterpillars to pieces of string that are glued to wooden dowels and start fishing for ducks! The ducks, once caught, make great favors.

TEDDY BEAR SONG SING-ALONG

YOU'LL NEED: Music

Structured game play is often overwhelming for little children, so sometimes it's best to let them come to a game on their own time. This easy sing-along is a perfect form of entertainment. The children sit in a circle with their bears and a cookie and sing teddy-bear-themed songs.

TEDDY BEAR HOKEY POKEY

This is the classic Hokey Pokey dance, made teddy bear specific! You should sing the song and direct the kids to put "your bear nose in" or "your bear paw in," following the lyrics of the classic song:

"You put your bear nose in, you put your bear nose out, you put your bear nose in and you shake it all about. You do the hokey pokey and you turn yourself around, that's what it's all about!"

Continue for a few verses, being creative with the body parts (ears! tails!).

beary friends picnic

TEDDY BEAR COOKIES

Oversized treats with brown fur sprinkles are sure to attract attention like honey to a bear!

1½ cups all-purpose flour
1   teaspoon baking powder
¼   teaspoon salt
½   cup unsalted butter
¾   cup sugar
1   large egg
1   teaspoon vanilla extract
1   batch vanilla frosting
     (recipe on page 140)
Brown sugar sprinkles
M&M's

In a medium bowl, sift together the flour, baking powder and salt. In a large bowl using a handheld mixer, beat together the butter and sugar until light and fluffy. Add the egg and vanilla and beat until creamy. With the mixer on low, slowly add the flour mixture.

   Gather the dough into a ball, cover it in plastic wrap, and let chill for at least one hour until ready to use.

   Preheat oven to 350°F. Divide the dough into thirds and remove one third; keep the remaining dough in the fridge until ready to use. On a lightly floured surface, roll the dough out to about ¼-inch thick. Using a bear cookie cutter, cut out bear shapes and transfer to baking sheets. Repeat with the remaining dough is used.

   Bake the cookies for 10–12 minutes or until light brown. Let cool before decorating.

   Frost cookies with vanilla icing, then immediately cover with a liberal coating of brown sprinkles. Add M&M eyes and buttons. Using a thin tip on a piping bag, place a small dollop for the nose. Place cookie on platter to allow icing to set. Continue with all cookies.

Picnic Menu

Beary Sandwiches

Carrot Sticks, Apple Wedges, and Orange Slices

Teddy Bear Cookies

Lemonade

Polka-Dot Cake

BEARY SANDWICHES

These are a simple but nutritious choice popular with little ones.

24 slices whole-grain bread
½ pound sliced deli ham
½ pound sliced deli turkey
½ pound bologna
Lettuce leaves
Mayonnaise

Make a variety of sandwiches with lunchmeats and lettuce. Use a bear-shaped cookie cutter to make bear-shaped sandwiches.

LEMONADE

6 cups cold water
2 cups granulated sugar
2 cups freshly squeezed lemon
   juice
4 cups ice cubes

In a drinks dispenser or large pitcher, combine the water and sugar, stirring until the sugar is dissolved. Add the lemon juice and stir until mixed. Chill until ready, then serve with ice.

beary friends picnic

POLKA-DOT LEMONY CAKE WITH LEMONY FROSTING

This is a citrusy twist on traditional butter cake. The polka dots I chose to decorate with are quite simple, but you can decorate as extravagantly as you desire.

2½ cups flour
1   tablespoon baking powder
½   teaspoon salt
¾   cup unsalted butter
1¾ cups sugar
3   large eggs, at room temperature
1   teaspoon vanilla
1   tablespoons lemon zest
1   teaspoon lemon extract
1⅓ cups buttermilk
¾   cup unsalted butter
3½ cups confectioners' sugar
1   teaspoon vanilla extract
2   tablespoons buttermilk, divided
2   teaspoons lemon zest
Yellow food coloring
Skittles

Preheat oven to 350°F. Butter and flour two 8-inch round cake pans. In a bowl sift together the flour, baking powder and salt. Set aside. In another bowl, using a handheld mixer, beat together the butter and sugar until fluffy. Add the eggs one at a time until well blended. Add the vanilla, lemon zest and extract, and mix well. With the mixer on low, add the flour in three batches, alternating with the buttermilk. Beat until blended but do not overmix. Pour the batter into the prepared pans. Bake 30–35 minutes or until golden brown and a toothpick comes out clean. Let cool 10 minutes. Invert baking pans onto plates and lift off baking pans. Let cool completely.

Meanwhile, make the frosting. In a bowl using an electric mixer on low speed, beat together the butter, sugar, vanilla and 1 tablespoon buttermilk until creamy. Add lemon zest, remaining tablespoon of buttermilk and one drop of food coloring. Mix until blended.

Place one cake layer on a platter or cake plate. Spread the top with frosting. Set the second cake layer on top and frost the entire cake with lemony frosting. Press Skittles into the frosting to cover the cake in polka dots.

medieval times
for knights and princesses

Castles, knights and princesses, oh my! This is a great,
broad party theme that appeals to both boys and girls, so it's perfect
for a mixed crowd. Charming knights and beautiful princesses
are happy to commingle in the perfect palace-land you have created.
So grab your crown and sword and let the games begin!

99

medieval ♜ times

Invitations

Have some fun by creating a scroll that really sets a regal tone. Water-color paper found in crafts stores is the perfect base for fancy computer-printed messages, such as "Here Ye, Here Ye, [Child's Name] has been summoned to a Royal Court to celebrate Sir Jack's 5th birthday. You are to appear before the Jester at 11 a.m. sharp on Tuesday, November 3."

You can roll it up and mail it in a small tube mailer, fold and mail in a flat envelope, or simply deliver it in person if your guests live nearby.

Setting the Scene

Set up the party space to feel like a grand hall in a castle with hanging flags and banners! We found the crests and flags by searching the Internet, and we then printed them and cut them out. The backdrop for the royal court space is cut from a large roll of purple paper found in an office supply store. The flags are embellished with fleur-de-lis stamps of glitter glue for an added majestic touch. Tape the flags onto your windows and walls for a stately look inside, or for an outdoor court, hang the backdrop on porch posts, railings or a fence.

Silver bowls filled with jewels and treats are truly fit for nobility. Place a few around the party space so the kids can gather extra necklaces and gems, and indulge in a few treats while playing.

TO DO

Beforehand

- Make the backdrops and flags.
- Paint the cardboard shields, swords and capes.
- Craft the princess hats.
- Gather costumes from around the house or pick up extras at a party store.
- Bake and decorate the cake.

Day of

- Wrap the parcel prizes.
- Hang backdrops and flags.
- Mix up the Fruit Punch.

Supplies

FOR THE INVITATIONS
- Watercolor paper
- Computer and printer
- Tube mailers

FOR THE PARTY
- Rolls of craft paper in purple, green or blue
- Large sheets (11-by-14-inch) of construction paper
- Tape
- Fleur-de-lis stamps
- Poster paint
- Glitter glue
- Foamy sheets
- Pearl and gem notions
- Ribbons
- Cardboard to make shields and swords
- Capes
- Glitter paint pens
- Silvery mesh fabric
- Assortment of play necklaces and bracelets

medieval ♜ times

Party Time

Encourage attendees to dress in their courtly finest. Costumes can be as simple or elaborate as you like. We provided princess hats made from foamy sheets embellished in regal style with pearls, gems and fanciful ribbons. These make excellent take-home gifts as well.

There's no need for a full suit of armor—it would be too cumbersome, anyway! Cardboard shields make noble armor, and a cardboard sword is a valiant and safe alternative for the preschool set. We provided custom capes for each Sir Valiant; using a glitter paint pen we wrote each child's name on his cape, such as "Sir Jack." Small pieces of silvery mesh fabric make soft chain mail when tied loosely around the neck.

As the birthday prince sits on his throne—we used a comfortable bench for our party—with his nobleman at his right hand, he can receive birthday guests. The castle cake makes an excellent addition to the royal decor.

Game Time
PASS THE PARCEL

YOU'LL NEED: One grand prize; assortment of small prizes (one per player); wrapping paper; tape

I love this game and often have some version of it no matter the age group!

Wrap the grand prize. Layer a smaller prize on top of the wrapped parcel, and wrap the whole thing anew. Keep adding prizes to the outside of the package and wrap again, until all the prizes are incorporated.

Sit the kids in a circle and hand the wrapped parcel to a player. Start the party music (see page 142). Have the kids pass the package around the ring for a short while, then stop the music. The player who is holding the parcel unwraps a layer to reveal a prize to keep. Start the music up again and have the kids start passing the present again. Repeat until each player has unwrapped a small prize. For the grand prize, play and stop the music so that the last kid gets to open it!

SWEET RING TOSS

YOU'LL NEED: Plastic rings (from party store); tablecloth; candies and small prizes

Easy and great for little ones, everyone gets to cheer for their friends to get the rings on prizes.

In the middle of the party space, lay down a tablecloth. Set candies and small prizes around on the cloth. Each player gets 3 rings, which they toss onto the tablecloth. Any prizes that end up in a ring are theirs to keep!

Medieval Menu

Mini Meat Pies

Royal Snack Mix

Fruit Punch

Castle Cake

FRUIT PUNCH

64 ounces fruit punch

32 ounces unsweetened pineapple juice

2-liter bottle ginger ale

½ gallon rainbow sherbet

In a punch bowl, mix the fruit punch, pineapple juice and ginger ale together. Using a small ice cream scoop, scoop sherbet into small balls and add them to the punch. Serve immediately.

ROYAL SNACK MIX

Little nibbles for little hands. And depending what you put in it, it can be healthy too!

4   cups rice cereal (such as Chex)

2   cups bite-size pretzels

2   cups Goldfish cheddar crackers

1   cup raisins

½   cup dried cherries

½   cup chopped dried apricots or chopped assorted dried fruit

½   cup peanuts (if desired, barring any allergies)

½   cup M&M's

Mix all ingredients in a large bowl. Serve with small plastic cups or bowls.

MINI MEAT PIES

These are like little meals in pockets. Perfect for noble ones on the go!

1   package puff pastry, defrosted

1   package Jimmy Dean breakfast sausage

1   small onion

1   package frozen carrots and peas, defrosted

1   tablespoon olive oil

1   egg, beaten

Preheat oven to 350°F. On a lightly floured surface, roll out the pastry and cut it into 6-inch squares. Mix together the sausage, onion, peas and carrots. Place ¼ cup of the mixture in the center of each square, then fold the pastry over to form a triangle, pressing the edges together. Brush pastry with the beaten egg and transfer to a baking sheet. Bake for 20 minutes or until the pastry is golden brown.

medievel ♜ times

CASTLE CAKE

Made from basic cake shapes, this cake looks far more difficult to make than it is. Assemble and decorate it the day before, as it is time-consuming to make.

- 2 boxes cake mix (or a double batch of the recipe on page 140 or 141)
- 2 cans of vanilla frosting (or a double batch of the recipe on page 140)
- Fondant in gray, green and purple
- Food coloring in gray, green and purple
- Sugar cubes
- 4 sugar cones
- Purple sugar sprinkles
- Tootsie Roll candies

Bake four 8-inch-square cakes according to package directions or using recipe on page 140 or 141. Let cool. Divide frosting in half and dye one half gray. Set other half aside.

Slice off any domes on the cake layers so that they are flat. Place one cake layer on a serving board and spread with gray frosting. Place another cake layer atop it with more frosting. Finish the castle base with a third cake layer and frosting. Take the fourth cake layer and cut it into quarters. Use three of these squares, with frosting in between, as the central tower. Frost the whole cake in gray. Roll the gray fondant out into smooth sheets and cut out doors and windows with a sharp knife. Press these details into the frosting. To make the small stones surrounding the door and windows, take small pieces of fondant and roll them into stone shapes. For window accents, roll and cut small pieces of purple and green fondant, then press them into the frosting just below the windows. The stone accents along the ramparts are made by covering sugar cubes with gray fondant.

Dye one cup of the remaining frosting purple. Take sugar cones and coat them in purple frosting, then roll them in purple sugar to make the turrets. Press the cones into the corners of the cake. Dye one cup of the remaining frosting blue, and use it to make the moat surrounding the castle. Dye the remaining frosting green, and fill in the rest of the board with grass as shown.

Lay Tootsie Roll candies across the moat to form the bridge as shown.

a date with dinosaurs!

jurassic park

Dinosaurs ruled the earth for millennia before they went extinct. Kids' fascination with them has never been stronger. Children who love dinosaurs, especially younger children—both boys and girls—will love a party dedicated to these gigantic prehistoric creatures. Invite your young guests to bring their favorite toy dinosaurs with them from home to create a prehistoric wonderland and a guaranteed good time at their own big dig!

a date with dinosaurs

SCHEDULE

Duration:
Approximately 2 hours
(10 a.m.–12 p.m.)

10:00–10:30	Dig for fossils
10:30–11:00	Dino footprint game
11:00–11:30	Food and egg hunt
11:30–12:00	Cake

Invitations

Make invitations that look like an archaeologist's map. Download a map and print it out on paper with an antique finish, or create the old look by staining white paper with strongly brewed cold tea. (Let the paper dry fully before writing the invitation.) Pen details in black marker. Mark the map with the activities they'll enjoy, and declare "Come dig up some fun!"

Setting the Scene

For an indoor dig, create a cave-like setting by lining the walls with brown kraft paper. Paint a jungle motif using poster paints, with tree trunks in shades of brown and hanging vines in shades of green. Tape lengths of green crepe paper from the ceiling to mimic jungle vines. Outdoors, use the house as a backdrop or create a cave-like setting from a swing set or outdoor playspace. Whether indoors or out, a few stuffed dinosaurs or plastic ones help set the mood and give kids more to play with.

Party Time

Set up a dig for dinosaur fossils for all the intrepid explorers. Make the fossils in advance by stirring together the coffee grounds, cold coffee, flour and salt until well mixed. Knead the dough and then flatten it out onto the waxed paper, letting it be somewhat thick and lumpy. Cut irregular-shaped pieces and create impressions by pressing objects into the dough, such as dinosaur feet or bones. Place on a cookie sheet and bake in a preheated 250°F oven for 1 hour. Remove from oven and transfer to a cooling rack. Let dry fully overnight. Bury the completed fossils in a sandbox or big tub of popcorn, as we did here. Be sure to have the digging station in an area where it's easy to clean up the mess!

Give all the kids their own excavator hats so they can look and feel the part.

TO DO

Beforehand

- Bake the fossils.
- Make the dino eggs.
- Bake the cake.
- Paint the jungle scene.

Day of

- Tape up crepe paper vines.
- Pop popcorn for the fossil dig.
- Make Caveman Chips.
- Cut the veggies and prepare the platter.
- Mix up the Prehistoric Punch.

a date with dinosaurs

Game Time

DINO DIG

YOU'LL NEED: Pre-baked fossils; sandbox or tub of popcorn; small varied prizes

The main feature of a Jurassic party is definitely going on a dig. Any large tub or shallow box will do as the spot to explore. If your party is outdoors, a clean sandbox works great. If you don't have a sandbox or if you are hosting indoors, fill a large basin with popped popcorn. (Because our party was outdoors, any spilled popcorn was left for the birds!) Bury the fossils, small plastic dinosaurs, gold coins and any other small prizes in the sand, and let the kids all have a go. Be sure to bury plenty of prizes so that everyone gets a fair share. The kids get to keep anything they find, including the fossils you made.

EXPEDITION FOR THE EGGS

YOU'LL NEED: Homemade paper mache eggs filled with prizes

This is a fun expedition with a great end result! Hide the paper mache dino eggs in the garden as we did, or around your party room, if held indoors. Be sure to hide them well so the children have to search for them a bit. When an excavator finds an egg, he or she can rip it open to find the treasure within! (One egg per child, please.) These are easy to make and a budget-friendly goody bag. Here's how to make them:

These eggs need plenty of time to dry, so make them in the days before the party. Blow up 10 balloons, or however many eggs you need. In a medium bowl mix 2 cups craft glue with ½ cup water. Cut the old newspaper into strips, dip them into the glue, remove excess glue and press the strips onto a balloon. Continue until the balloon is covered, overlapping the glue-covered strips. Hang the balloon to dry by the knot in a well-ventilated area. Repeat with all the balloons, then let dry 12 hours or overnight. Once dry, cut a small slit in each egg big enough to insert treats and wrapped candies. Tape the slit closed, then paint the eggs dino brown. Let dry.

FOLLOWING THE FOOTSTEPS

YOU'LL NEED: Paper dinosaur footprints; music; small prizes and one bigger prize

This is a version of magical chairs tailored to a dinosaur theme! Cut out dinosaur footprints (see template at in the back of the book) from brown kraft paper. Make one fewer footprints than there are children at the party. Lay them in a circle on the lawn. Start the music and have the children dance around the footprints. When the music stops, they must find and step on a footprint. With each round, one child and one footprint is eliminated. Have small prizes on hand for the children that get eliminated each round, and a bigger prize for the winner.

a date with dinosaurs

CAVEMAN CHIPS

1 package tomato-flavored
   flour tortillas
1 package whole-wheat flour tortillas
Cookie cutters in the shapes of bones
   and footprints (or use templates
   at the back of the book)
Vegetable oil
Sea salt

Cut out bone and foot shapes from
the tortillas. Heat ½ cup oil in a
shallow pan on medium high heat
until very hot: a tiny piece of tortilla
dropped in the oil should sizzle
immediately. Place 3 or 4 shapes at
a time in the oil for 1–2 minutes,
flipping once, until crispy. Remove
from oil and place on paper towels
to drain. Salt lightly with sea salt.
Serve with Caveman Dip (see next
recipe).

Jurassic Menu
Caveman Chips
Caveman Veggies and Dip
Dino Nuggets
Prehistoric Punch
Dino Cake

CAVEMAN VEGGIES AND DIP

1 cup salsa
½ cup lowfat sour cream
Carrot sticks
Celery sticks
Sliced bell pepper

In a small bowl, mix salsa and sour
cream. Serve with veggie sticks and
Caveman Chips (see previous recipe).

PREHISTORIC PUNCH

16 ounces limeade
16 ounces lemonade
2 drops green food coloring
4 cups ice

Mix the limeade, lemonade and
food coloring in a plastic drink
pitcher. Add ice and serve.

DINO NUGGETS

Dinosaur-shaped chicken nuggets
Prepare the specialty-shaped
chicken nuggets according to the
package directions. If you can't find
dino-shaped, plain nuggets are fine.

DINO CAKE

1 dinosaur cake pan
1 box cake mix (or recipe
   on page 140 or 141)
1 can icing (or recipe
   page 140 or 141)
Green food coloring
Skittles candies

Preheat oven to 350°F. Butter and
flour the pan, being careful to cover
all corners and surfaces. Prepare
the cake mix following the box or
the recipe on page 140 or 141. Let
cool. Remove from pan and place
on a cutting board or heavy
cardboard covered in aluminum foil.

   Mix green food coloring with the
icing one drop at a time until the
frosting is your desired shade of
green. Frost the cake fully with the
frosting, then use candies to
decorate as shown in the photo.

114

splish ✳ ✳ splash
sprinkler ✳ fun

You don't need a swimming pool to make a splash. A sprinkler party is a great way to beat the heat and celebrate a birthday! Start with lots of blue and green decorations, add a menu inspired by sea life, and top it off with some fun water play, all of which will result in happy water bugs!

splish splash

SCHEDULE

Duration:
Approximately
2 hours (12–2 p.m.)

12:00–1:00	Water games
1:00–1:30	Lunch and games
1:30–2:00	Cake and games

Invitations

Go for something fun and simple that your birthday boy or girl can help with. Cut simple fish shapes from blue and green cardstock, then write the invite information on the fish. Say something splashy like "Come cool off!" or "Let's make some waves!" Be sure to remind everyone to bring a bathing suit and towel.

Setting the Scene

This is a party that must be held outdoors, so plan it for a warm day and get the yard ready! Blue and green decorations are a great color scheme: buy balloons, streamers and paper lanterns to hang from trees or patio awnings in those colors to make a festive backdrop. Set up a sprinkler and keep the hose handy for lots of splashy fun. Water pistols and small buckets add to the entertainment, and if you have a Slip 'N Slide waterslide, there's almost no need for other games! Beach balls are colorful and inexpensive, so blow up a bunch and toss them about. If you can find one, a bubble machine that releases glistening bubbles into the air will make the party even more memorable.

TO DO

Beforehand

- Gather supplies for crafts.
- Gather inflatables such as beach balls and tubes.
- Get a bubble machine.
- Make Fishbowl Jell-O.
- Bake cupcakes and assemble cones.

Day of

- Set out sprinkler, bubble machine and toys.
- Make sandwiches and biscuits.
- Mix limeade.

Supplies

FOR THE INVITATIONS
- Cardstock in blue and green
- Scissors
- Markers

FOR THE PARTY
- Hoses
- Sprinklers
- Slip 'N Slide
- Beach balls
- Water pails

splish splash

Party Time

Start out with games and water play, and then have kids towel off for lunch and birthday cake-cones. Set the table with buckets full of chips and veggie puffs, pinwheels and candies. Place the party table in a shady spot under a tree or porch awning to give the children a break from the sun and a breather from the energetic games they're playing.

The cake cones were inspired by a summer staple, soft-serve ice cream. The polka-dotted cones are hiding cupcakes under swirls of frosting!

Game Time

WATER BALLOON TOSS

YOU'LL NEED: Balloons filled with water; small prizes

Have all the kids pair up and give one member of each pair a water balloon. Line up the kids with partners facing each other about 2 yards apart. Say "Ready, set, go," and have the partners toss the balloon back and forth. They keep tossing as long as they catch it, but one bad move and the balloon will pop, dousing one member of the team and putting that pair out. The last pair with an intact balloon wins!

SPONGE BRIGADE

YOU'LL NEED: Four buckets, two filled with water, the other two empty; two large sponges; small prizes

Mark the empty buckets at the same spot, about three-quarters of the way up the side. Divide the children in 2 teams and have each team form a line. Place a filled bucket in front of each team, and about 4 yards away place the empty buckets. Drop a sponge in each of the buckets of water and let it get saturated. Call out, "On your mark, get set, go!" and the first player from each team will grab the sponge, race to the empty bucket, and squeeze the water out. A quick dash back to the full bucket, and it's the next kid's turn. The teams keep going until one team hits the line on the previously empty bucket, and they are the winners!

HULA HOOP CONTEST

YOU'LL NEED: One hula hoop per child; small prizes

The beach is the place to hula! This hula-hooping contest with have all the kids in the swing.

Put on some classic surfer tunes, like the Beach Boys or the theme to *Hawaii Five-O,* and give each child a hula hoop. On "Go!" everyone starts hooping. If they drop the hoop, they're out—last one still hooping wins!

WATERMELON EATING CONTEST

YOU'LL NEED: Watermelon; small prizes

This is as hilarious to watch as it is fun for the kids!

Cut large wedges out of the watermelon, one per guest, and place them on the table. Gather the children and have them stand around the table in front of their plates. On the count of three, the kids start eating—without using their hands! The first one to finish is the winner. This is a messy, drippy, sticky game, so send them off to the sprinkler to clean up right after!

splish splash

FISHY SANDWICHES

These fish-shaped grilled cheese sandwiches are convenient to snack on during breaks from the fun!

3   tablespoons butter, divided
32 slices whole-grain bread
16 slices American cheese

Place a griddle pan over medium heat and add 1 tablespoon butter to coat pan. Make 6 cheese sandwiches using 2 slices of bread and 1 slice of cheese. Place the sandwiches the on griddle and cook for 4–5 minutes per side or until golden brown. Repeat with remaining butter, bread, and cheese until 16 sandwiches are prepared. Use a fish-shaped cookie cutter to make fish grilled cheese sandwiches!

Splashy Menu
Fishy Sandwiches
Starfish Sweet Potato Sticks
Fishbowl Jell-O
"Ice Cream Cone" Cupcakes
Limeade

STARFISH SWEET POTATO STICKS

These good-for-you veggie sticks make great finger foods.

6   sweet potatoes
4   tablespoons olive oil
½   teaspoon sea salt

Preheat the oven to 450°F. Wash and peel the sweet potatoes. Cut in half lengthwise and then cut the halves into ½-inch strips. Arrange on an oiled baking sheet, drizzle with olive oil and sprinkle with salt. Bake for 30 minutes, flipping once, or until the edges turn crispy and light brown. Serve warm or at room temperature.

FISHBOWL JELL-O

Gummy fish swimming in a bowl of Jell-O is a magical treat for kids!

2   packets blueberry flavored Jell-O
12 gummy fish

Wash and dry a new unused fishbowl or large, clear glass bowl. Prepare the Jell-O according to package directions and pour it into the bowl. Let it start to set in refrigerator for about 10–15 minutes, then remove while a thick liquid (like egg whites). Use a knife to push the gummy fish down into the bowl, placing each fish at a different height. Return the bowl to the refrigerator to set fully, overnight. Keep chilled until ready to serve.

LIMEADE

1   cup freshly squeezed lime juice
     (about 6 limes)
8   cups water
1   cup sugar
4   cups ice cubes

Mix the lime juice, water, and sugar in a pitcher. Serve over ice.

splish✲splash

"ICE CREAM CONE" CUPCAKES

With no risk of melting, these "ice cream cone" cakes are fun and tasty!

- 1 batch vanilla cupcake batter (recipe on page 140)
- 2 batches vanilla frosting (recipe on page 140)

Sprees candies
12 wafer ice cream cones
Jelly beans

Preheat oven to 350°F. Prepare the vanilla cupcakes until the batter is mixed. Line a 12-cup muffin pan with paper liners. Line a 16-cup mini muffin pan with paper liners. Pour the batter into the muffin cups, to about ¾ full. Bake the mini cupcakes for 15–18 minutes and the regular-sized cupcakes for 20–25 minutes, or until a toothpick inserted in the center comes out clean. Let cool 10 minutes, then remove cupcakes from the pans onto a baking rack to cool completely.

Prepare a double batch of the vanilla frosting recipe on page 140. Remove the papers from the cupcakes. In the bottom of a wafer cone pour about 10 jelly beans, primarily for weight and stability but also as a fun surprise! Take a regular cupcake and push it gently into the cone top-down; the bottom will stick out about an inch. Place a dollop of frosting on the cupcake and place a mini cupcake, also top-down, into the icing, so that it tapers. Repeat with all the wafer cones.

Transfer the remaining frosting to a pastry bag fitted with a star tip. Starting at the edge of the cone, pipe a generous spiral of frosting around the cupcakes and even higher, mimicking soft-serve ice cream. Gently press candies into the frosting.

GOODY BAGS!

It's always fun to send the kids home with something after a party. For this party, it's fun to decorate tote bags and fill them with plastic sunglasses, goggles, bubbles and sunscreen! Buy simple canvas totes at a crafts store and embellish them with fabric paint and ribbon in nautical themes.

truck
rev your engine
rally

Rev up your engines—it's truck time! Trucks are such a huge part of childhood play, and this is a great party to showcase little ones and their big rigs. A truck party works perfectly as a coed theme, as little girls love to play with trucks, too!

truck rally

SCHEDULE

Duration:
Approximately 2 hours
(10 a.m.–12 p.m).

10:00–10:30	Decorate hats
10:30–11:00	Games
11:00–11:30	Obstacle course and play
11:30–12:00	Lunch and cake

Invitations

A bright yellow card with "muddy" truck tracks running all over it instantly tells the invitees about the theme of the party. Dip the wheel of a toy truck in black acrylic paint and roll it over a piece of yellow cardstock. Use wording such as: "Make tracks over to [Birthday Child's Name]'s garage for truckloads of birthday fun!" and remind them to bring their favorite truck to the party to play with!

Setting the Scene

The centerpiece to this party is the massive truck tunnel. It takes some time to construct, and it is messy work, but the payoff is immense. It's like a large paper mache tunnel: Wrap a large box with a tunnel cut out of it in chicken wire. Soak strips of newspaper in a mixture of equal parts glue and water, and drape the strips over the chicken wire. No need to keep it smooth: Lumps and bumps make it look more like solid rock! Once the tunnel is completely covered in paper, set it to dry overnight. When dry, paint it with gray and brown acrylic paint and let dry fully. Add some neon construction signs, bought at a local hardware store, for spectacular signage and set the tunnel in the middle of the play area. Set some signs on wooden dowels and stand them up in the grass.

To be sure all the kids have a vehicle to play with, whether they brought one from home or not, I

TO DO

Beforehand

- Construct the tunnel.
- Make the signs.
- Plan the obstacle course.
- Clear the sandbox and bury prizes.
- Paint tracks on the cloth and goody boxes.
- Bake cake.

Day of

- String caution tape and set up the obstacle course.
- Make Pizza Rolls.
- Mix up Truckers' Brew.

scattered play trucks around the yard. "Work Zones" were created by race courses, the truck tunnel, digging in the sandbox, and an obstacle course. Caution tape strung here and there brought authenticity to the party site.

Supplies

FOR THE INVITATIONS
- Yellow cardstock
- Toy truck
- Black paint
- Markers

FOR THE PARTY
- Caution tape
- Toy trucks
- Utility signs (from a hardware store)
- $3/8$-inch wooden dowels
- Glue
- Yellow tablecloth
- Toy truck
- Black paint
- 6 plastic or foamy construction hats
- Stickers with truck themes
- Small takeout containers
- Yellow party "grass"
- Stickers and candy

Tunnel
- Large cardboard box
- 3 yards chicken wire
- Glue
- Newspaper
- Brown and gray acrylic paint
- Paintbrushes
- Plastic drop cloth

truck rally

Party Time

The tablescape filled with truck tracks is a "snack zone" for the busy truckers to take a break and also serves as a work table when the party begins. A bright yellow plastic tablecloth painted with truck tracks (like for the invitations) fits right into the theme. Small takeout boxes filled with goodies make good take-home gifts.

As the kids arrive to the party, give them a plastic hard hat and sit them at the table, which is piled with stickers that they can use to personalize their hat. Later they can sit at the table for snacks and cake, after running the obstacle course or playing in the sandbox!

Game Time

TRUCK RACES

YOU'LL NEED: Small orange plastic cones; trucks; small prizes

Set small orange plastic cones out to designate a starting line and a finish line about 4 yards away. Line the children and their trucks up at the start and call out "On your mark, get set, go!" Have them roll their trucks along the ground to the finish line—first one across the line wins! Play this game more than once to give kids plenty of chances to win.

SANDBOX PLAY

YOU'LL NEED: Clean sandbox; small prizes

Before the party, clear the sandbox of all other toys and bury small prizes such as trucks, play cones, or truck accessories in the sand. Let the children dig them out with small shovels and backhoe trucks. They can take home all their finds!

OBSTACLE COURSE

YOU'LL NEED: 1 20-pound bag of sand; 2 gallon buckets or containers; 2 small buckets; a 12-inch-by-4-foot piece of wood for plank; 2 cement blocks or bricks; 2 hula hoops; small prizes

Position a pile of sand at one end of the play area, and the large containers at the other. Set out obstacles, like a plank across cement blocks, hula hoops as "holes," and anything else you want, between the two areas.

Divide the children into two teams and provide each team with a small bucket. Gather the teams near the empty large buckets. When you say "GO!" the first child on each team must run over the plank, hop over the hula hoop to the pile of sand, avoid any other obstacles, then fill the bucket with sand. The kids then have to come back through the obstacle course to the empty bucket and pour their sand in. The first team to fill its bucket wins!

truck rally

MINI FRUIT KABOBS

1 cantaloupe
½ small watermelon
1 pineapple

Cut the cantaloupe in half and scoop out the seeds. Dice the fruit into chunks, removing the rind. Cut the watermelon up into chunks in the same way. Remove the rind from the pineapple and cut it into pieces the same size as the melon. Thread the fruit onto bamboo skewers and serve.

TRUCKERS' BREW

1 32-ounce bottle cranberry juice
1 cup freshly squeezed lemon juice
1 cup freshly squeezed orange juice
1 cup sugar
1 liter lemon-flavored seltzer
4 cups ice cubes

In a large bowl, mix the cranberry, lemon and orange juices together. Whisk in sugar. Pour the mixture into a serving pitcher about ¾ full, top off with the lemon-flavored seltzer and serve with plenty of ice.

Truckers' Menu

Pizza Rolls
Mini Fruit Kabobs
Truckers' Brew
Dump Truck Cake

PIZZA ROLLS

Add fillers such as broccoli, onions, fresh tomatoes, peppers or mushrooms to get some vegetables in.

2 batches fresh or frozen pizza dough
16 ounces tomato sauce
4 cups shredded mozzarella cheese

Preheat oven to 425°F. On a lightly floured surface, roll the pizza dough out with a rolling pin until it is about ¼-inch thick. With a sharp knife, cut the dough into 6-inch wide strips. Spread tomato sauce onto the strips, leaving a half-inch border, sprinkle mozzarella cheese atop, then roll the strip up into a spiral. Place the rolls seam-side down on a baking sheet and bake for 25 minutes or until golden brown. Let cool, then cut into bite-sized pieces and serve.

DUMP TRUCK CAKE

Serve this cake in the back of a clean plastic dump truck for the coolest party fare around!

1 batch chocolate cake (recipe on page 141)
3 cups pre-made chocolate pudding
1 16.6-ounce package Oreo cookies, crushed (save a few for garnish)

Butter and lightly flour a 9-by-13-inch cake pan. Bake cake according to directions on page 141. Let cool completely, then cut into 3-inch squares. Place a layer of the cake squares in the bottom of a clean dump truck lined with plastic wrap. Spoon a layer of pudding over the cake squares, then top with a layer of crushed Oreo cookies. Top with more cake squares, pudding and crushed Oreos. Garnish with reserved whole Oreos and serve with a plastic shovel!

strike up the band

super sing-along

Most young children love music, and little kids are uninhibited
enough to sing and play an instrument to their hearts' content
in front of others. It's clamorous good fun.

super sing-along

SCHEDULE

Duration:
Approximately 2 hours
(11 a.m.–1 p.m.)

11:00–11:30	Maraca making
11:30–12:00	Sing-along
12:00–12:30	Lunch and games
12:30–1:00	Cake and play

Invitations

To keep it all in the right key, use blank sheet music folded up to form the invitation. Write on the front lines with a colorful marker something like "Strike Up the Band, It's [Child's Name]'s birthday, let's make some noise!" List the details on the inside of the card.

Setting the Scene

Musical notes, a few bursts of color and comfy cushions are all you need to decorate the room; the space will soon be filled with singing and music instead!

Cut musical notes (see templates at the front of the book) from sheets of poster board, then coat them in a thin layer of glue and a good coating of glitter. Shake off the excess and let dry. Hang the notes around the party space. I hung paper sunbursts found at a party supply store from the ceiling to add to the merriment.

Baskets filled with play instruments are joined by handmade drums, which are best made in advance. Take empty, clean oatmeal canisters with their lids and decorate them with sheets of construction paper and shapes cut from foamy sheets. Cover the top and bottoms with a circle of aluminum foil, attach a long piece of cotton lacing so the drum can hang from a kid's neck, and the kids can tap their fingers on the drum's top to work the percussion section!

TO DO

Beforehand

- Craft the musical notes.
- Make the drums.
- Gather supplies for maracas.
- Burn the CDs.
- Make the place mats.

Day of

- Decorate the party space.
- Set out cushions.
- Prep the food and drink.

Set the table with "Happy Birthday" place mats help to keep messes small while providing a fun visual. They are easy to make and create a ready-made going-home treat. Find the sheet music for "Happy Birthday" online and print it out. Cut colorful music notes out of construction paper using the template (mentioned previously) and glue them around the music. Bring this finished mat to a copy shop and have copies made and laminated!

Supplies

FOR THE INVITATIONS

- Blank sheet music
- Markers in various colors

FOR THE PARTY

- 10 sheets 22-by-28-inch white poster board
- Scissors
- Glue
- Foamy paint brush
- Glitter in various colors
- Paper sunbursts
- Tape
- Play instruments

Place Mats

- "Happy Birthday" sheet music
- Black marker
- Construction paper

Drums

- Oatmeal canisters emptied and wiped clean
- Construction paper in bright colors
- Adhesive-backed foamy shapes in bright colors
- Aluminum foil
- 4 yards bright green cotton lacing
- 1 foamy sheet
- Double-sided tape

Maracas

- 8 12-ounce water bottles, washed and dried with labels removed
- Pony beads in bright colors
- 6 yards bright green cotton lacing
- Foamy beads in assorted colors

super sing-along

Party Time

Start the party off by making musical instruments together. Maracas are fun and easy to make. Give out empty water bottles and lots of plastic beads. Let the kids fill the bottles as much as they want—more beads will make a different sound than fewer beads. Help them to glue the caps on by dabbing a bit of glue into the threads. Tie a string around and add more beads for an extra touch.

When the instruments are completed, have the children sit around the comfortable cushions and sing their favorite songs, such as "Old MacDonald Had a Farm," "London Bridge" and "Twinkle, Twinkle Little Star." Encourage them to play along however they see fit with instruments they made or found in the basket. When their little bodies get restless, play a lively game of musical chairs and freeze dance. Instead of a formal goody bag, have a grab bag full of prizes. After each game, the winner is invited to dive in and pick his or her prize.

The music doesn't stop playing when it's time to eat. Keep a CD playing of favorite kid songs—in fact, burn extra copies of this CD and give them out, in pretty packaging, as a favor! Gather around the cake made to look like a drum and belt out "Happy Birthday" for all to hear!

Game Time

MUSICAL CHAIRS

YOU'LL NEED: Chairs; music

Gather chairs in a circle with the seats facing out. Assemble as many chairs as there are children at the party. As you play the music, the children walk or skip around the chairs. Stop the music and let each child find a seat and sit down. For the first round, everyone will find a chair; this assures the game gets off to a fun start. For the subsequent rounds, take one chair away. The child left standing is out. The last one to get a seat wins!

FREEZE DANCE

YOU'LL NEED: Music

This is a good choice of a fun, energy-filled game. Play upbeat music and let them dance around. Stop the music and everyone freezes in the exact position they are in! So long as there is no music, they must be still. Anyone who moves is out. Start the music up again, let them dance around, then stop it suddenly! Keep going until only one tiny dancer is still going.

super sing-along

PINWHEELS

10 whole wheat, tomato or spinach tortillas
½ cup cranberry sauce
½ cup mayonnaise
½ pound deli ham
½ pound deli turkey
½ pound Swiss cheese
1 cup chopped lettuce

Make an assortment of wraps using the tortillas, condiments, lunchmeat, cheese and lettuce. Roll them up in a spiral and slice them into 1½-inch round. Set the pinwheels on a platter, and keep an eye on the kids as they eat so that the toothpicks don't get in the way.

RICE CRACKERS WITH HUMMUS

Store-bought rice crackers are a healthy alternative to chips. It's all about the dip anyhow!

1 15-ounce can chickpeas, drained
Juice of 1 lemon
2 tablespoons light olive oil
1 garlic clove, peeled and chopped
1 teaspoon sea salt
Rice crackers

Combine the chickpeas, lemon juice, olive oil, garlic and salt in a food processor and blend until smooth. Spoon into a bowl and serve with the rice crackers.

Sing-Along Menu
Pinwheels
Rice Crackers with Hummus
Watermelon Quarters
Drum Cake

DRUM CAKE

2 batches vanilla or chocolate cake (recipe on page 140 or 141)
3 cups confectioners' sugar
1 cup (2 sticks) butter
1 teaspoon vanilla extract
2 tablespoons heavy cream
Blue food coloring
White and red fondant
Air Heads candies
Strawberry Twizzlers
Pirouette cookies

Preheat the oven to 350°F. Butter and lightly flour three 8-inch cake pans. Prepare the cake batter according to directions on page 140 or 141 and pour it into pans until ¾ full. Discard extra batter. Bake according to directions or until a toothpick comes out clean. Let cool in pans for 10 minutes, then invert cakes onto a baking rack to cool completely.

Meanwhile, in a bowl with an electric mixer, beat together the sugar and butter. Mix on low speed until well blended and then increase speed to medium and beat for another 3 minutes. Add the vanilla and heavy cream and continue to beat on medium speed for 1 minute more, until the buttercream is light and fluffy. Divide the frosting into two bowls. Add 2 drops blue food coloring to one bowl and mix well.

Place the bottom round layer in the center of a large piece of cardboard covered in foil. Coat the top with a layer of white buttercream. Place another cake layer atop the first and add a layer of white buttercream. Set the last layer on top and cover with a generous layer of white buttercream. Using an offset spatula, frost the sides of the cake with blue buttercream. Roll the white fondant about ¼ inch thick and cut it into a circle using a cake pan as a template. Set the circle atop the cake. Decorate the sides of the cake like a drum using Air Heads as trim and licorice as lacing. Make cake-topping drumsticks by rolling balls of red fondant into circles and pressing long pirouette cookies into them.

standard recipes

Although boxed cake mix and purchased frosting has become increasingly popular with the modern mom, making a cake from scratch really doesn't take that long, it tastes delicious, contains only ingredients that you control, and it's worth the extra trouble to be able to say, "I made it myself."

Vanilla Cake

This is a standard, basic cake that's always a crowd-pleaser!

2¼ cups all-purpose flour
1   tablespoon baking powder
¼   teaspoon salt
¾   cup (1½ sticks) unsalted butter, softened
1¾ cups sugar
2   teaspoons vanilla extract
3   large eggs
1½ cups whole milk

Preheat oven to 350°F. Butter and flour your chosen pan(s), whether two 8-inch round, two 9-inch round, or one 9-by-13-inch. Tap out excess flour.

In a bowl sift together the flour, baking powder and salt. Set aside. In a large bowl using a handheld mixer or standing mixer with a paddle attachment, beat together the butter, sugar and vanilla until smooth. Add the eggs, one at a time, beating well after each egg. Add the flour mixture in three additions, alternating with the milk and blending until smooth.

Refer back to the party recipe at this point to determine if there are specific next steps, or else pour the batter into cake pan(s), dividing it evenly if using more than one pan. Bake on the middle rack of the oven for 25–30 minutes if using 2 pans, 30–35 if using 1 larger pan, until golden brown or until a toothpick inserted in the center comes out

clean. Cool in pan(s) for 10 minutes. Invert on wire racks and let cool completely.

Makes two 8-inch round cakes, two 9-inch round cakes, or one 9-by-13-inch cake.

Vanilla Frosting

¾   cup unsalted butter, softened
3¼ cups confectioners' sugar
2   tablespoons heavy cream
2   teaspoons vanilla extract
¼   teaspoon salt

In a bowl using an electric mixer or standing mixer with a whisk attachment on low speed, beat all ingredients until creamy and a bit fluffy, about 4 minutes.

Vanilla Cupcakes

Cupcakes are the perfect thing for a kid's party, because one portion is enough to satisfy little partiers! Make extras for the parents who help out, too.

1¼ cups all-purpose flour
1¼ cups cake flour
1   teaspoon baking powder
½   teaspoon salt
1   cup (2 sticks) unsalted butter, softened
1¾ cups sugar
1   teaspoon vanilla extract
3   large eggs
¾   cup whole milk

Preheat oven to 350°F. Line two 12-cup muffin pans with paper liners.

In a bowl stir together the flour, baking powder and salt. Set aside. In a large bowl using a handheld mixer or standing mixer with a paddle attachment, beat together butter, sugar and vanilla until creamy, about 3 minutes. Add the eggs one at a time, beating well after each addition. On low speed, beat in the flour mixture in three additions, alternating with the milk. Beat until blended.

Scoop the batter into the muffin pans, filling each about ¾ full. Bake 18–20 minutes or until golden brown and a toothpick inserted in the center comes out clean. Let cool in pan for 10 minutes, then remove cupcakes from pan and cool completely on a wire rack.

Makes 24 cupcakes.

Chocolate Cake

Use a good unsweetened cocoa powder such as Valrhona or Ghirardelli.

1 **cup unsweetened cocoa powder**
¾ **cup hot water**
1¾ cups all-purpose flour
1 **teaspoon baking soda**
¼ **teaspoon salt**
1 **cup (2 sticks) unsalted butter, softened**
1 **cup light brown sugar**
¾ **cup granulated sugar**
3 **large eggs, at room temperature**
2 **teaspoons vanilla extract**
¾ **cup buttermilk**

Preheat oven to 350°F. Butter your chosen pan(s), whether two 8-inch round, two 9-inch round, or one 9-by-13-inch. Cut a piece of wax paper to fit the bottom of the pan(s), then line the pan(s) with the wax paper, butter the paper, and dust the pans with flour or a bit of cocoa powder. Tap out excess flour or cocoa powder.

Place the cocoa powder in a medium bowl. Add the hot water and a whisk until smooth. Let cool.

In a large bowl using a handheld mixer or standing mixer with a paddle attachment, beat together the butter and sugars on medium speed until creamy, about 2 minutes. Add the eggs, one at a time, beating well after each. Add the vanilla and mix well. Slowly pour in the chocolate and beat until blended.

Add the flour mixture in three additions alternating with the buttermilk, beating until blended after each addition.

Refer back to the party recipe at this point to determine if there are specific next steps, or else pour the batter into cake pan(s), dividing it evenly if using

more than one pan. Bake on the middle rack of the oven for 25–30 minutes if using 2 pans, 30–35 if using one larger pan, until golden brown or a toothpick inserted in the center comes out clean. Cool in pan(s) for 10 minutes. Invert on wire racks and let cool completely.

Makes two 8-inch round cakes, two 9-inch round cakes, or one 9-by-13-inch cake.

Chocolate Frosting

½ **cup heavy cream**
8 **ounces unsweetened chocolate, chopped**
4 **ounces bittersweet chocolate, chopped**
1 **cup unsalted butter, softened**
2¾ **cups confectioners' sugar**
2 **teaspoons vanilla extract**

Place the heavy cream in a heatproof bowl set over a saucepan of simmering water. Add the chocolates, stirring occasionally until melted and smooth, about 5 minutes. Set aside to cool.

In a bowl using an electric mixer or standing mixer with a whisk attachment on low speed, beat the butter and sugar. Beat in the vanilla, and slowly pour in the chocolate until combined. Beat until light and fluffy, about 2 minutes.

Chocolate Cupcakes

1¼ cups cake flour
1¼ cups all-purpose flour
½ **tablespoon baking soda**
½ **teaspoon baking powder**
¼ **teaspoon salt**
½ **cup unsweetened cocoa powder**
½ **cup boiling water**
1 **cup (2 sticks) unsalted butter, softened**
1¾ **cups sugar**
1 **teaspoon vanilla extract**
3 **large eggs**
¾ **cup whole milk**

Preheat oven to 350°F. Line two 12-cup muffin pans with paper liners.

In a bowl sift together the flours, baking powder and salt. Place the cocoa powder in a small bowl and add the boiling water. Stir until smooth.

In a large bowl using a handheld mixer or standing mixer with a paddle attachment, beat together the butter, sugar and vanilla on medium speed. Add the eggs one at a time, beating well. On low speed, beat in the flour mixture in three additions, alternating with the milk. Beat until blended. Stir in the chocolate mixture until incorporated completely.

Scoop the batter into the muffin pans, filling each about ¾ full. Bake 20–22 minutes or until a toothpick inserted in the center comes out clean. Let cool in pan for 10 minutes, then remove cupcakes from pan and let cool completely on a wire rack. Makes 24 cupcakes.

resources

You're likely to find many of the materials you need to host these parties around your house, and you can find the rest at your local office supply store or party store. Here are some companies with multiple locations as well as online ordering to serve all your party needs.

A.C. Moore
www.acmoore.com
Faux florals, paper and paper crafts, framing materials, seasonal decorations and children's crafting supplies.

A.I. Friedman
www.aifriedman.com
Faux florals, foam sheets, felt, baking supplies, paper crafts and framing supplies.

Dick Blick Art Supplies
www.dickblick.com
Variety of art supplies including, paint, canvas and brushes.

Dick's Sporting Goods
www.dickssportinggoods.com
Wiffle balls and bats, baseball bases, other balls and toys.

Dylan's Candy Bar
www.dylanscandybar.com
Large variety of confections from old-fashioned candies to a rainbow assortment of modern-day favorites.

Jo-Ann Fabric and Craft Stores
www.joann.com
Arts and crafts supplies, paper, cards, fabric, scrapbooking materials and more.

Kate's Paperie
www.katespaperie.com
Stickers, stamps, paper-crafting supplies, ribbon, wrapping papers and specialty papers.

Kohl's
www.kohls.com
Children's tights, tops and T-shirts.

Michaels
www.michaels.com
Kid crafts, kits, yarn, fiber crafts, floral decorations, seasonal decorations, framing supplies, and scrapbooking and baking supplies. (No online ordering.)

M & J Trimming
www.mjtrim.com
Ribbons, sequined trim, beaded trim, decorating appliqués.

NY Cake and Baking Supplies
www.nycake.com
Cookie cutters, shaped and novelty cake pans, bakeware, doilies and decorative sugars.

Oriental Trading Company
www.orientaltrading.com
Party supplies and treat-bag fillers.

Party City
www.partycity.com
Party supplies such as balloons, cups, plates and napkins, as well as themed supplies.

Pearl River
www.pearlriver.com
Asian-inspired paper and floral garlands, lanterns and decorative accessories.

Staples
www.staples.com
Office supplies and basics like glue, tape, scissors and more.

Target
www.target.com
Tops, ballerina slippers, tights, T-shirts and a large selection of party supplies.

music

Playing music at a party makes free playtime even more fun, encouraging movement, dancing and even singing along! This is a list of some great kid-friendly albums.

THE BEST OF THE LAURIE BERKNER BAND, Laurie Berkner
YOU ARE MY SUNSHINE, Elizabeth Mitchell
CATCH THAT TRAIN!, Dan Zanes
HOT POTATOES, THE BEST OF THE WIGGLES, The Wiggles
150 FUN SONGS FOR KIDS, The Countdown Kids
PRINCESS DISNEYMANIA, Various Artists
JUICE BOX HEROES, Imagination Movers
JUNGLE GYM, Justin Roberts
THE BASICS, Ralph's World